# Nonfiction Literacy

## Ideas and Activities

# Gretchen G. Courtney • Sarah A. Jossart

**KENDALL/HUNT PUBLISHING COMPANY**
4050 Westmark Drive     Dubuque, Iowa 52002

Book Team

Chairman and Chief Executive Officer    Mark C. Falb
Vice President, Director of National Book Program    Alfred C. Grisanti
Editorial Development Supervisor    Georgia Botsford
Developmental Editor    Tina Bower
Vice President, Prepress Services    Chris O'Brien
Prepress Services Manager    Kathy Hanson
Prepress Editor    Shelly Ansel
Permissions Editor    Renae Heacock
Cover Design Manager    Jodi Splinter
Cover Designer    Suzanne Millius
Senior Vice President, College Division    Thomas W. Gantz
Vice President and National Field Manager    Brian Johnson

# ontents

*We would like to dedicate this book to all of the colleagues*
*we have worked beside in the field of education.*

# About the Authors

From her early years the "how-to's" and the "why's" always fascinated Gretchen Courtney. School was her mecca for this trait. In third grade, she wanted to study anthropology and joined a group at school that went to the University of Chicago for classes. Fourth grade was her year of discovering biographies, the "how-to's" and "why's" of lives of famous people.

This trait has persisted in all phases of her life—including helping others learn. Gretchen is an educational consultant in St. Charles, Illinois.

Sarah Jossart's love for nonfiction text goes back to her early education days in a one-room school on the North Dakota prairie. "I read every book I could find on Babe Ruth, Amelia Earhart, Clara Barton and the Titanic. Today, I am still intrigued by these subjects and many more." Sarah is a reading specialist and has taught students of all ages. She lives in Elgin, Illinois, with her husband and family.

*Nonfiction Literacy* is the fourth book co-authored by Gretchen and Sarah. *Story Dramas: A New Literature Experience for Young Children, Story Dramas for Grades 4–6: A New Literature Experience for Children* and *Celebrate Literature* are previous publications published by Good Year Books and Perfection Learning Corporation.

Dear Colleagues,

*Nonfiction Literacy* was written to share with you the joys of reading, writing, listening and speaking about nonfiction text. Included in this informational resource book are suggestions for selecting text, short introductions to a few nonfiction authors, ideas to meet the needs of diverse students and ways to teach reading through nonfiction text. Chapters on questioning techniques and graphic organizers present ways to help students comprehend nonfiction text. The following sections give extensions of nonfiction text through drama, art, Internet and written response. Finally, chapters on writing nonfiction and evaluations conclude this teacher-to-teacher resource book.

The world of nonfiction information is vast. Consider the following facts. All of them are true except one. Do you know which one is false? There are no snakes in Ireland and New Zealand. The heart has twenty-five trillion red cells, more than the stars of the Milky Way. There are sixty-thousand miles of blood vessels in the human body. A female naked mole rat can give birth to 90 pups in her twelve-year life span. (The answer is found on the bottom of the page.) Reading nonfiction text gives information and insights into the world around us. Some facts may be important, some are interesting and still others are strange and weird, but these facts are available to readers and listeners of nonfiction text. We promise that adventures into nonfiction literacy will be a learning experience for everyone.

*Gretchen and Sarah*

(The female mole rat gives birth to 900 pups in her life span.)

# Introduction

## Looking at Nonfiction Text and Selection

*Breathtaking Noses, Wormology, The Amazing Pop-Up Grammar Book and Seven Wonders of the Historical World* are examples of the overwhelming number and variety of nonfiction texts available to students and teachers. No other genre of children's literature has exploded with new publications at the same rate as nonfiction text. Traditionally, nonfiction text was referred to as reference materials, characterized by big, heavy books with lots of print and a few black and white illustrations. This is no longer true. The genre of nonfiction literature is quickly taking its place on library shelves, filling these shelves with brilliantly illustrated books discussing fascinating topics. This rapidly developing genre has publications produced in a variety of presentation formats covering a vast amount of topics.

Teachers and students are devouring nonfiction books. Students, especially boys, are requesting to read nonfiction text for pleasure. Nonfiction text satisfies curiosity about the real world. It expands the students' knowledge base, increases their vocabulary, and promotes inquiry and creative thinking.

The role of nonfiction text is important in everyone's lives. All people depend upon accessing knowledge and using nonfiction text. Students need to learn how to use, read and write nonfiction text to meet the demands of the world around them.

With the prolific supply of nonfiction text inviting readers to explore, students and teachers alike are faced with the task of selecting the best books for classroom use as well as independent reading. Evaluation of nonfiction text is an important skill for all users of nonfiction.

## Defining the Genre of Nonfiction

The traditional definition of nonfiction literature is factual informational text that explains, reports, persuades, recounts or provides procedures. The content of nonfiction text today provides information about our world, people, animals, and experiments as well as activities pertaining to factual subjects. This genre also provides meaningful explanations of concepts. The information gained in reading nonfiction text helps us understand the world around us. It offers knowledge of the past and present as well as predicting the future. Today's nonfiction entertains.

Today's nonfiction text is presented in a variety of formats. There are picture books, activity books, documents, how-to-books, photographic essays, ABC books, journals and even pop-up-books. There are books for browsing and books for deeper study. Nonfiction text is also available on CD-ROM.

Nonfiction text has changed its face in other ways. Many of today's nonfiction books are being written as a series. In these series, each book focuses on a specific subject. For example, you can find a series with books about each planet rather than a book about space or a series about individual insects versus a book on insects. Students like books found in series because they have consistent formats. Once students have been introduced to the series' format, they are comfortable reading other books in the series. Students know what to expect while reading, how difficult the text is going to be, what text structure is being used and what role illustrations play in the understanding of the text. For these reasons, series are a motivating factor for reluctant nonfiction readers. Some of the series that are popular with intermediate students are the *Creepy Crawly Collection* (Gareth), *Secrets of the*

*Animal World* (Gareth), *Living Spaces* (Rourke), *Eye Witness* (Darling Kindersley), *Mysteries of Science* (Millbrook), *Make It Work* (Thomson Learning) and *Weird and Wacky Science* (Enslow).

Along with the more traditional nonfiction text is the publication of nonfiction text with voice. The voice of the author comes through in the way the author gives information. The reader readily discovers the author's purpose and identity. This type of nonfiction literature can be best described by looking at a few examples. Shonto Begay's book, *Navajo*, is a collection of poetry describing the different aspects of life by a Navajo through the author's own personal experiences. The voice of the poet sharing his culture is evident in this piece of nonfiction literature. Donald Graves' first book of poetry, *Baseball, Snakes and Summer Squash*, is an autobiographical look at his early years. These poems are taken from Grave's childhood journal, and his voice is present in these poems.

*I Spy Spooky Night: A Book of Picture Riddles* by Jean Marzsollo is text written in riddle form that shares the humor and playful voice of the author. Authors can be identified through humor. Autobiographies and journals, such as the account, *Zlata's Diary: A Child's Life in Sarajevo*, by Zlata Filipovic and *A Desert Scrapbook*, by Virginia Wright-Frierson are first person narratives of the author's observations and experiences. First person accounts can only be read through the eye of the writer. We see, feel and hear what the author wants to share with us.

# Guides for Evaluating Nonfiction

## Accuracy

There is no set order of criteria when selecting nonfiction text but certainly one of the most important selection criteria is accuracy. Nonfiction texts must present information that is accurate. Teachers and students cannot be experts in all areas and therefore rely on editors and authors to present information accurately. There are several ways to check for overall accuracy of a text. A current copyright date will help ensure accuracy. In quickly changing areas, such as space exploration and advancement in technology, new and updated information puts some texts out of date almost before the books become part of a library's collection. However, the latest nonfiction literature book will almost always be more current than a classroom textbook covering the same topic.

Cross-checking information is also helpful when you are concerned about getting accurate and up-to-date information. Cross-checking can be done by looking at several sources to confirm information. These sources can include other pieces of literature, newspaper articles, magazines and Web sites. Cross-checking information is a valuable lesson in critical reading for students and is a very worthwhile activity for students to learn.

**Remember**

➡ Check for current copyright date

➡ Cross-check to reveal accuracy of text

➡ Check for major references cited

➡ Check that concepts are not oversimplified

Finally, look for major references cited as sources of information in writing the nonfiction text. Check to see if the author has used primary sources, information gained from their own experiences or expertise, or secondary sources, information gained through research. The sources cited can give the reader confidence in the accuracy of the text.

## Labeling and Illustrations

Illustrations, drawings, photographs, maps, timelines, diagrams, cutaways and other artistic works are all means of visual information used to highlight or extend the text. Consider the information presented in the labeling of these illustrations when you are evaluating nonfiction text. Quality illustrations support the accompanying text. The illustrations should be labeled, and the reader should

know at a glance which caption goes with what illustration or which part of an illustration is being pointed out and labeled. The illustration and accompanying text should also be on the same page or side-by-side pages for easy reference.

## Language

Each text should also use language that does not offend the reader. Correct identification of ethnic groups and identification of countries are two examples of areas that need to be addressed correctly.

Correct technical language should be used as well. For example, text about the human body should use correct physiological terms unless an appropriate synonym is more familiar. The use of collarbone instead of clavicle is an acceptable synonym. Selecting nonfiction text that uses correct and accurate language will benefit students not only in their present learning but also in their understanding of the world around them. Students who learn accurate terms can transfer that learning to new learning and situations later in their lives.

Evaluate the text for biases. This evaluation is especially important when selecting biographies. Look for text where the author makes no judgments about the main character in the biography, but rather presents enough points of view that the reader can draw his/her own conclusions about the individual. This unbiased approach is also an important issue when selecting books that cover subjects of controversy.

Avoid scientific text that uses anthropomorphism, which is the application of human feelings and behaviors to animals and plants. While personification works in fiction it does not have the same effect in nonfiction text for older students. Anthropomorphism may be more acceptable in factual text for young children or for students who have had little experience reading nonfiction and need to be introduced to the genre in a more familiar format. Generally, the use of human feelings and behaviors in nonfiction text should be avoided.

## Authority

When selecting nonfiction text, critically examine the information about the author. If the author is not a recognized expert in the field, check to see if the author cites the sources of information used to write the text. Good writers will site their sources somewhere in the text. Check the Foreword, Afterword, Acknowledgments and About the Author for this information. Some recognized contemporary nonfiction authors are Seymour Simon, Russell Freedman, Gail Gibbons, Aliki, Joanna Cole, Millicent E. Selsam, Jean Craighead George, Jean Fritz, Jerry Palotta and Avi.

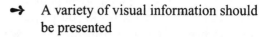
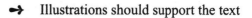

**Remember**

→ Illustrations should support the text

→ A variety of visual information should be presented

→ Illustration should have accurate and precise labeling

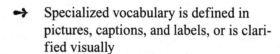
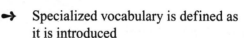

**Remember**

→ Specialized vocabulary is defined as it is introduced

→ Specialized vocabulary is defined in pictures, captions, and labels, or is clarified visually

→ Specialized vocabulary is in a glossary

→ Correct technical language is used

→ Language is culturally accurate and bias free

→ Language is appropriate for textual organizational structure

**Remember**

→ Author should be a recognized expert in the field

Or

→ Author should cite sources of information

## Thoroughness of the Content

As you select nonfiction text it is important to look at the depth at which a subject is covered. Your objective for using the text is an important point to consider. If the content of the selected nonfiction literature is to supplement a textbook, you need a more in-depth look at the subject. If however, your objective is to introduce students to a new topic or concept, a less thorough text may be adequate. Check to make certain facts that are important to the subject are not omitted. For example, a book about an animal should include information on the life cycle or reproduction aspect as well as habitat, eating habits, enemies and so on.

**Remember**

➜ Check that all areas pertinent to the topic are covered, avoiding irrelevant topics

➜ Pictures and text should represent both genders

➜ Biographies need to include the entire person's life

Biographical nonfiction should demonstrate the aspects of the whole person. In addition to the person's accomplishments and achievements, the lesser biographical incidents that make the individual human should be recorded. Today's biographies often focus on a period of years instead of the whole life of an individual. Depending upon the use of the text, this is important for the reader to know when making a biography selection.

## Attractiveness and Organization

The content of the text should be organized and presented in an interesting way. The mixture of illustrations and text should be appealing and not too busy. The text should develop from simple to more complex by connecting familiar concepts with new or lesser-known concepts.

**Remember**

➜ Mixture of illustrations should be appealing but not too busy

➜ Text should develop from simple to more complex text, connecting concepts

➜ Text has a predominate pattern of organization

➜ Text includes table of contents, index, graphics, chapter and section headings and glossary

## Appropriateness

In making nonfiction selections for classroom use, teachers are encouraged to keep a balanced amount of texts chosen for read-aloud, shared reading, guided reading, browsing, research as well as independent reading. The books selected should extend and enhance the grade level's curriculum rather than provide the curriculum.

Consider the appropriateness of the nonfiction text for classroom use. Subjects once thought to be taboo or controversial issues are being published. *Weird and Wacky Science* text series may be accepted while a book on another topic such as the Aids virus might be unacceptable. Check the district's policy on use of supplementary materials. Be prepared to share your purposes for selecting any supplementary text.

**Remember**

➜ Text should include appropriate subjects

➜ Text uses appropriate format including number of pages and print size

➜ Text has positive role model for gender, age, disabilities and ethnicity

➜ Suggested activities are motivating

## Check for Additional Sources

Look for additional reference aids provided by the author for extending learning, questioning and exploring. A glossary, index, and table of contents are important additional aids found in many factual texts. Other reference aids to look for are: bibliography of more books about a subject, a list of places to write to find out more about a topic, maps and or charts to extend the information of the text and places to visit. Look for activities to do as individuals or groups, experiments, questions for adult and child interaction, where to shop for items, list of related videos, places to visit to observe the subject, Web sites, as well as quizzes to check for understanding of the text

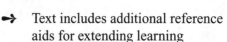

### Remember

→ Text includes additional reference aids for extending learning

→ Text includes a bibliography of additional titles

→ Text references a list of places to find out more information concerning the topic

→ Text provides questions for adult and child interaction

→ Assessment techniques are included in the text

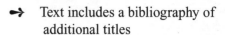

## Conclusion

The best advice in selecting nonfiction texts is to spend time browsing through and reading nonfiction text. Teachers and students alike are encouraged to spend time exploring the nonfiction sections of the school and public libraries. This allows teachers and students to appreciate the variety of text content as well as formats and styles. Students learn to enjoy the genre of nonfiction literature when engaged and immersed in the reading of the genre. Teachers should make a conscious effort to read nonfiction orally to model the variety of texts available. Through the teacher's oral readings the students can be directed to the best nonfiction books available.

# Using Nonfiction Text: Meeting the Needs of All Students

One of the great challenges for classroom teachers is to provide materials and instruction that meet the needs of all students. The great variance in the literacy development of students is part of this challenge. It is not unusual to have emergent readers and writers in intermediate grades. Nor is it unexpected to have fluent readers and writers performing at grade levels beyond their intermediate grade placement. Changes in special education and educational policies require students with special needs be placed in the least restrictive environment, the regular classroom. In addition, classrooms have students from varying cultural backgrounds. Teachers need to recognize these differences and provide learning experiences that support each student as a learner.

Every student comes to school to be challenged and supported as a learner. Schools must meet these academic needs as well as the students' interests. One assignment in reading and writing for all students is not appropriate instruction. By varying assignments for students and giving them choices, students are successful in reading and writing, and finding relevancy in what they are reading and writing. Integration of language arts activities into information units of study assists students in making connections. All learners benefit when instruction allows for choices and is integrated across curricular areas.

In classrooms, it is possible to establish classroom practices and activities to meet the needs of students. The following classroom practices and classroom activities are ideas for meeting the challenges of diverse classrooms.

# Classroom Practices

## TRADE BOOKS USAGE

Nonfiction trade books are available to support many intermediate content areas as well as the theme units used in intermediate grades. Students who are struggling to read content area textbooks can often gather information with more ease from trade books. Trade books support curricular concepts. Nonfiction trade books are less threatening and are more attractive. Trade books are rich in detail with imaginative formats. They keep the students' interest by being more focused and often go into greater depth about a subject. An author sharing his interest in a topic is motivating to students when compared to the voiceless words in a content textbook. Reluctant readers of nonfiction find trade books to be rewarding reading.

Bringing a few trade books into the study of curriculum content areas offers the opportunity to provide reading materials at different reading levels. Books on tape or CD-ROM are other options for the emerging or second language reader.

Exposure to a variety of informational sources encourages students to read for the purpose of learning. Nonfiction text enriches student understanding of content areas by adding new information, stating information in different ways and exposing students to repeated use of the content's special vocabulary.

## BUILD BACKGROUND KNOWLEDGE

The background information students bring to nonfiction text has a great influence on their comprehension. Helping students build and increase their background knowledge is one way teachers meet the needs of all students. Background knowledge is increased by:

- Reading to the students about the topic of study.

- Allowing time for students to browse through books.

- Providing visual and auditory information through the use of the Internet, TV or video.

- Using hands-on activities.

- Guest speakers.

- Reading primary sources.

- Pre-reading discussion and brainstorming.

- Questioning.

- Shared reading.

## READ ALOUD

When some students are unable to read nonfiction text, the teacher can read the text aloud in order that all students have access to the important concepts of the text. Student readers can be used if they are good models of oral reading and have had a chance to practice the text before the presentation. Reading aloud to students and follow-up discussions help students internalize the text's language patterns and content. Content vocabulary is read in context helping students flush out meaning. In return, read-alouds help when students reread text. In some situations, an important concept is only present in one text. If this text is too difficult for every student to read, then reading aloud meets the needs of those students.

Reading aloud can be used to build students' interest, give samples of nonfiction content and expose students to different formats used by nonfiction authors. Inviting parents, community and school personnel to read to students models the importance of literacy skills for everyone.

## USE SHARED READING TO MODEL THE READING AND WRITING PROCESSES

A nonfiction book can be used to model the reading and writing processes of informational text. Show students how to read and write nonfiction text through modeling. During the modeling lesson, the teacher focuses on the needs of students in the class by selecting skills and strategies needed by the students for success with nonfiction reading and writing. As the teacher models, reading and writing skills are reinforced and new concepts are introduced. At times, small groups meet for additional modeling lessons. A modeled reading lesson may include:

- inferring from text

- how to summarize text

- accessing of prior knowledge/making connections

- previewing/predicting text

- questioning before, during and after they read

- thinking about vocabulary the author might be using in the text and how to learn new vocabulary

- accessing print

Each reading strategy or skill presented during a modeled lesson is discussed with input from the students as well as the teacher. Students may share some of their readings that illustrate the modeled lesson. Modeling by the teacher benefits all students, for example, modeling how to use textual clues and connections to make inferences.

Big books work well for modeling. Overhead transparencies and projected text through a scanner to a TV monitor also work well. By using enlarged text and illustrations all students have access to the print through both visual and auditory means, helping many students who are not strong in these areas.

Big books are also used for models of nonfiction writing. A modeled writing lesson may include:

- discussion of the format

- leads used in nonfiction writing

- structure of nonfiction writing

- use of illustrations and captions

- how to add detail and support to nonfiction text

- author's craft and the way the author keeps the readers' interest in the text alive

By keeping a posted list of all the different techniques authors use, students can refer to this listing when they are writing nonfiction, for example, through the use of humor and illustrations, text formats, overlays and points of view.

## GIVE STUDENT CHOICES

Students choose books to read on a theme, topic or unit of study. When giving a writing assignment, include more than one option for completing the assignment and allow students a choice. These choices might include topic selection as well as the choice of format: narrative, poem, letter and so on. When students are given choices, they are participating in the learning process. They are able to access and use prior knowledge to comprehend or write nonfiction text. Students also take ownership in assignments and invest more effort in the processes of reading and writing. The more opportunities students have to make choices, the better they become in making choices to meet their needs.

## PLAN LESSONS FOR ALL LEARNERS

Planning lessons with many types of assignments and activities meets the needs of different students. For example, some students are more attentive and motivated to express themselves more when the activity is language centered. Others will excel in a performing situation like plays, pantomimes and scripted dialogues. Still other students can express themselves best in creative ways such as illustrations, paintings, dioramas and sculpture. Listed are a few examples of the activities and assignments to consider for students who express interest in different areas: storytelling, oral presentations, experiments, illustrating, role-playing, problem solving, writing, personal goal setting, researching and the use of technology and music. In addition, these activities can be completed in groups or by individuals to meet the needs of students who prefer to work collaboratively or individually.

At times, students are working in areas less comfortable to them, but by providing variety students find areas in which they can excel while learning new ways to think. When planning lessons or activities, think of adaptations to the assignment so all student learning can be Supported.

## ASK OPEN-ENDED QUESTIONS

Focus on asking and modeling questioning with questions that have multiple possible answers. Open-ended questions have many possible answers so they invite all levels of students to participate and become active learners. These types of questions are also effective with students for whom English is a second language. Try the following questions to provide open ended questions to use with nonfiction text. (See Chapter Three for more on questioning.)

- What do you think…?
- Why did…?
- What would you do if…?
- How do you think…?
- Why do you think…?
- When will you…?

- Why not?
- How will…affect you?
- How might you use this information?
- What information has meant the most to you and why?
- What have you learned? What do you want to know?

## READ HISTORICAL AND REALISTIC FICTION

Some students need to bridge the gap of narrative literature to nonfiction reading. Encourage students to read historical and realistic fiction to provide a bridge into the reading of nonfiction. Reading historical and realistic fiction with a unit of study creates interest and inquiry. These reading experiences encourage readers to seek out nonfiction text for accurate information. When students are reading historical fiction books about the Civil War, they find accurate information about the war. This type of interaction fosters students' interest in a battle, a region of the United States or an important figure. This interest then leads the way to additional nonfiction reading on the topic.

## CONFERENCE WITH STUDENTS

Conferencing with students is a very effective way to meet nonfiction literacy needs. A conference targets the exact needs of each individual student. This is a time for students to talk about learning while the teacher listens. It is also a time when students are instructed on basic skills needed for reading or writing. For example, in a writing conference the teacher focuses on the writing process, giving the student time to discuss his/her writing and then selects with the student what further help is required to continue writing. Each conference will be unique to the needs of the student.

## READ MULTICULTURAL LITERATURE

The availability of multicultural literature meets the needs of all students. Students of different cultural backgrounds are personally encouraged when reading about people that share their background and their contributions to society. While reading multicultural literature, all students learn about different traditions, values and customs. They gain knowledge of regions, geography and history of different cultures. Encourage students to read books by and about a wide range of cultural backgrounds.

# Classroom Activities

## TEXT SAMPLING

Choose books that are part of a theme, topic or unit of study. Put students in small groups of two or three. Give each group a book to discuss. After the small group discussion, each group records their discussion in illustration form on chart paper. Display these charts with the books in the classroom to promote interest. Then by allowing students some time to look at the text and evaluate them, they are able to make better selections to meet their own needs when asked to pick a book to read on the topic. The following questions can be used in the discussion.

- How would you describe this text?
- In what format is the text written?
- What words do you think are needed to read this text?
- What do you think you need to know before reading this text?
- Will the text be easy or difficult to read? Why?
- To whom would you recommend this text and why?
- What strategies would you use with this text? Why?

## DISCUSSION GROUPS

There are several different formats for discussion groups: literature circles, novel and interest groups and book clubs. In these groups, all students share their ideas about nonfiction text and explore new ideas. Because these groups are smaller in size, many students feel more comfortable discussing their ideas.

## STORY DRAMA

The nature of story drama activities allow for participation by every student in the classroom because there is no right or wrong response. Each student is valued as an active participant in the drama as it unfolds and is given the chance for a successful experience. Story drama is highly motivating for most students and builds interest in the text. See Chapter Five, page 47 for an explanation of how to use story drama.

## LEARNING LOGS OR JOURNALS (SEE CHAPTER SIX, PAGE 63.)

## COOPERATIVE LEARNING

Students are put in a group to learn and often produce a final product. Competition is not present, but rather each member is expected to contribute to the group. All members share the responsibility for learning and for leadership. Emerging readers are supported in groups when others read the text. For those students who are less informed about a topic, the group helps them use the vocabulary, explains and reinforces concepts. Students who understand the concepts are given the chance to put their knowledge to work while explaining illustrations and communicating their knowledge.

## CURRICULUM JIGSAWING

At the intermediate level, every student may not be able to study and read every possible assignment. In curriculum jigsawing, the curriculum is divided into sections and assigned to small groups of children. These divisions can be student selected or teacher assigned. Each group brings back a "piece of the puzzle" by sharing what they have learned. For example, while studying explorers, students choose which explorer they wish to research. After each member has done his research, they report back to the whole group. These reports may be done in many formats: an oral report, written report, mini role-playing of the characters, illustrations, display and so on. With the use of technology, students can create interesting presentations using audiovisual techniques on the computer. Jigsawing gives every student access to all the information.

## FISHBOWL DISCUSSIONS

A small group of students form a circle in the center of the room to discuss a nonfiction text or topic. The other students are outside the circle as observers. First this small group discusses the text or topic for 10 to 15 minutes. Then the students outside of the circle respond to what they have heard discussed. This activity meets the needs of all students. Those students in the "fishbowl" are informed, articulate and knowledgeable about a subject. They are students who volunteer freely and have good information to share. After listening to the discussion of the content and the reinforcement of specific vocabulary, those students who are less informed or knowledgeable about a topic are more prepared to contribute to a group discussion.

## In Conclusion

Each classroom practice and activity discussed is only a starting point. The best teaching involves adaptation and development of new activities to meet the needs of all students. Educators are continually challenged to motivate, immerse, instruct and engage all students in the use of nonfiction text.

# Reading Nonfiction Text

## Introduction

Most of the reading that people do in life is nonfiction, yet in intermediate classrooms, reading instruction focuses primarily on the study of fictional novels. Instruction in the classroom needs to be balanced between reading in both genres: fiction and nonfiction. The ability to read and understand nonfiction is a necessary skill for students who live in an information age.

An effective reader of nonfiction text knows when to access nonfiction material, what type of material to use, how to most effectively process the printed text as well as how to locate and evaluate information. These critical thinking skills are essential for all students, helping them through their educational years and preparing them for careers. While reading, students need to continuously employ a set of strategies, using them so fluently that the ebb and flow of strategic thinking moves the reader effortlessly through a piece of nonfiction text. Students need to know how to make predictions, ask questions, identify the organization of text, grapple with complex vocabulary, continuously summarize, make inferences and determine textual relationships. Students need to make conclusions about textual information and support their decisions with logical evidence and examples from many sources. As a result of reading, students need to construct accurate and appropriate generalizations that apply in a variety of situations.

The genre of nonfiction literature is diverse, including classroom content area texts as well as the most innovative informational books. In the intermediate grades, students are introduced to a wealth of informational material. Often students settle for reading fictional series, even though they prefer nonfiction, but find it challenging. Students who have been instructed in the technique of reading nonfiction feel comfortable pursuing nonfiction text. They are adept information seekers, willing to select reading material from a broad range of possibilities. This chapter is devoted to the creation of voracious, dedicated nonfiction consumers.

## Promoting Nonfiction Reading

In classrooms where inquiry is an integral part of the curriculum, a diverse selection of nonfiction materials is displayed and accessible. Students are immersed in the unique features of nonfiction material and are well on their way to becoming versatile nonfiction readers. There are many ways to promote nonfiction reading in classrooms:

- Give nonfiction book talks

- Read the newspapers and news magazines aloud

- Have nonfiction author studies

- Form book groups around nonfiction topics

- Purchase classroom subscription of magazines written for intermediate children

# Content Area Classroom Textbooks

Traditional textbooks offer many challenges for the nonfiction reader. Pictorial and graphic notations include much of the written information. Challenging vocabulary and new concepts slow the reader's pace and often interfere with the process of constructing meaning. The organization of the text varies, often within the same text, sometimes on the same page. These structures demand a fluid, flexible approach from the reader. Teachers need to explicitly teach the skills and strategies necessary for fluent reading of content area textbooks. Shared reading experiences, small group-assisted reading lessons, as well as focused independent practice reading nonfiction materials comprise a well-developed approach for the instruction of content area reading.

The curricular demands of an intermediate classroom encroach on the time allotted to the teaching of reading. The use of a large group and shared reading experiences provide the optimal use of time when introducing a concept directly taught to all students. Shared reading is directed by the teacher working with a large group of students exploring ideas and demonstrating problem-solving techniques with text. During shared reading time, students are introduced to new and different ways to read. For shared reading lessons, teachers model skills and techniques using large size texts (most publishers offer the big book format for intermediate grades), or text displayed on overhead transparencies. Shared reading lessons provide a solid beginning for the long learning process from introduction of a strategy to mastery. The teacher uses this introductory step to teach skills and strategies, assist learning and evaluate students' application of skills. Shared reading lessons can be used to introduce any new concept. Many of the possibilities are listed below:

- How to activate prior knowledge

- How to acquire vocabulary

- How to apply word study techniques in context

- How, when and why to adjust reading rate

- How to use text structure to predict and confirm

- How to summarize content

- How to connect known information to new information to enhance meaning

- How to draw conclusions

- How to generalize information to a variety of situations

Shared reading lessons are successful because the teacher constantly reminds students what they are doing, why they are doing it and how it helps them become better readers. After assisted and independent practice using these strategies, students are able to articulate their own reasons for and reactions to the process for reading nonfiction text. Shared reading lessons do not need to be lengthy to accomplish this task. Fifteen to twenty minutes is adequate to demonstrate a concept and discuss it in a group setting. When the piece of text being used in shared reading is from the unit of study, the textual information is being digested along with the reading procedures.

Content area texts have many specialized features. These features provide signposts for readers. The illustrations, graphics, captions and titling alert readers that they need to notice this important information. These special features clarify and extend the text, offering information when concepts are abstract or outside students' prior knowledge and experience, often giving them the visual representation needed to understand nonfiction text. Students need to pay special attention to the following:

- Illustrations, drawings and photographs

- Graphics, diagrams, tables, charts, cross-sections, overlays

- Index, preface, table of contents, glossary

- Transitions that clue the reader to take notice (for example, in fact, in conclusion, more important, therefore)

- Fonts, titles, headings, bold print, italics, bullets, labels

## GRAPHIC EXAMINATION ACTIVITY

1. Display only the graphics of a piece of nonfiction text.

2. Read the graphics, noting the key words and phrases.

3. Ask students to list the ideas they anticipate the author will cover in the text.

4. Read the text of the piece together. Using the students' list of anticipated ideas, abandon those not accessed. Assimilate or accommodate ideas the author does address into the list.

5. Review the list of revised information found in the text. Point out to students that these ideas are the main ideas of the text.

6. Review the steps in the process: Anticipate, Abandon, Assimilate, Accommodate.

## NONFICTION PREDICTING ARROW

1.  Have the students examine the illustrations, graphics and captions to determine what topics they expect to read about.

2.  Have the students write facts or information that they expect to read about in the Expect boxes.

3.  As students read, they record textual information in the boxes under Expect box, which is related to the information.

4.  If the textual information is a new concept for the students, the word "new" is highlighted. If the concept is familiar to a student and similar to what they already know, the word "similar" is highlighted.

5.  As students read, they may discover information they did not expect to read. Record this information in the Unexpected Boxes.

### Predicting

| **Expect** problems | **Expect** times/dates | **Expect** destruction | **Expect** return with |
|---|---|---|---|
| men left to go to spain  (new)  similar | Sept. 1493  (new)  similar | fort/destroyed new settlement  (new)  similar | slaves  new  (similar) |
| islanders - mad  (new)  similar | 2 years - another voyage  (new)  similar | new  similar | new  similar |
| | Puerto Rico | Cuba | never on U.S. | |

**Unexpected**

### Predicting

| **Expect** fault | **Expect** tectonic plates | **Expect** shifts | **Expect** stress |
|---|---|---|---|
| transform boundary  new   similar | smooth move friction  new   similar | rifts red sea - a rift  new   similar | transform connection cells  new   similar |
| predicting earthquake  new   similar | new   similar | failed rift  new   similar | new   similar |
| | predicting earthquake | safety tips | | |

**Unexpected**

## NONFICTION TEXT PREVIEW

1. Prior to the reading of informational text, organized in a textbook format, students complete the text preview organizer by surveying the text and recording the highlighted information in their own words. Rewriting the text-based information requires students to organize and structure the information, thus setting the stage for meaningful reading.

2. Students refer to the organizer while reading text, adding connections, ideas or additional questions.

# Text Preview

**Lesson/Section Heading(s)**

How Rome was formed.

**Captions**

They were skilled in many forms of art.

**Bulleted Items**

How the Etruscans lived and worshipped.

What their tombs were like.

**Graphic Information**

Rome is located on the west side of Italy.

**Guiding Questions**

What jobs did the Etruscans have?
What is the social order?

**My Focus for Reading**

How did the Etruscans become such a civilized group of people?

**Bold Print**

gladiatorial games were part of their lives / they had a city government

| 1 | 2 | 3 | 4 |
|---|---|---|---|
| No evidence of understanding or completely erroneous. | -Some/all sections fairly complete<br>-May or may not be in student's own words, when important<br>-Limited evidence of understanding | -All sections complete—some may be sketchy<br>-In student's own words, when important<br>-Some evidence of understanding | -All sections complete<br>-In student's own words when important<br>-Shows evidence of understanding |

# Nonfiction Text and Trade Books

There are important differences between narrative fiction and nonfiction text; differences in structure, style, content and purpose. Most intermediate students are comfortable and knowledgeable fiction readers. Nonfiction text does not fit into schema students have developed for fiction. Nonfiction informational text introduces unfamiliar topics, factual material and new structures of organization. There are four basic qualities of nonfiction text that distinguish it from fictional text:

- Nonfiction text does not necessarily indicate a person reference in the writing, narrative is usually written in first or third person.

- Nonfiction text is organized and connected in many ways whereas narrative text is usually written in chronological order.

- Nonfiction text is mostly an explanation of the content and fictional text represents the action of characters.

- Nonfiction text is written in a variety of tenses; narrative text is frequently written in past tense, the retelling of events.

Identifying and utilizing text structure is one of the most important variables in the comprehension of nonfiction text. Grappling with text structures assists readers in determining essential ideas. When students are able to recognize how information is presented in the text it helps them recall and synthesize the important concepts. Failure to use expository text structure has a greater negative effect on learning when the topic is unfamiliar. Considering these premises, teachers need to take an active role in providing explicit instruction for identifying text structure to improve comprehension.

## Nonfiction Text Structure Sentences

Allow students to explore the differences and similarities between the different text structures by having them write a different sentence using the same word or phrase, to represent each type of text structure. For example:

- **Definition/example**—Spectrums of light are produced in many ways. The rainbow is one example

- **Timeline/chronology**—In the early 1800s, the first prism was used to reflect a spectrum of light in scientific experiments. By the early 1850s, the use of rainbow-colored light produced by prisms was being used for many scientific as well as medical purposes.

- **Description**—A rainbow is a colorful spectrum of light stretching from the ground to the heavens.

- **Cause and effect**—Rainbows are formed by the effect of sunlight shining through water droplets. When the sun breaks through the clouds, the light reflects the spectrum of light off the surface of the water droplets producing a spectrum of color.

- **Enumeration**—Rainbows often appear after thunderstorms. First, the rain tapers off producing a haze of water droplets. Then rays of light reflect off the water producing a colorful spectrum.

- **Compare and contrast**—Rainbows are considered beautiful acts of nature by some. Others believe that rainbows are magical pathways to a pot of gold.

- **Question and answer**—What happens when sunlight shines through rain? A rainbow appears.

- **Problem and solution**—The rainbow-colored oily patches on the wet highway were hazardous for automobiles until the Tire Right Company developed the first nonslip, double-traction tire tread.

See Chapter Four for additional ideas for the instruction of text structure analysis.

Along with cracking the complex code of text structure organization, students also face the daunting task of determining the meaning of words and concepts they don't understand. Unusual or difficult content-related vocabulary can interfere with fluency while reading. Accessing prior information about complex textual vocabulary, as well as using context to extract meaning, are effective systems for vocabulary acquisition.

## NONFICTION TEXT IMPRESSIONS

This activity draws the students' attention to the important textual vocabulary of the selection, requires students to use their prior lexical information and asks students to predict textual information prior to reading. After completing this activity, students recognize which words are important, know the contextual definitions and are able to reject or confirm their expectations of the information.

1. Prior to the reading of nonfiction text, select words from the text that may challenge students, but also are important to the meaning or message of the text.

2. List the words in the order they occur in the text on a piece of paper and distribute the lists to students.

3. Ask students to write or tell what they expect to learn in the text. They should use the words from the list in order.

4. Have students read the text noting how the author uses the words and information presented.

5. After the text has been read, have students write a summary of the information actually presented in the text using the initial list of words to guide their writing.

## MAGNET WORDS

The following context-related vocabulary exercise not only provides students with a successful way to interpret the meaning of words, but also incorporates an effective summarizing technique promoting ongoing comprehension.

1.  While reading a piece of nonfiction, have students look for the first informational paragraph.

2.  Have students "map" the detail words and phrases on the outside of the magnet.

3.  Have students consider the details and decide on a key point that is related to the details.

4.  Point out to students that if the key point they selected is actually a magnet (key idea) word, their map will be extensively supported with words and phrases from the paragraph.

5.  After students have identified the magnet words from several consecutive paragraphs, have them weave the magnet words and phrases from the paragraphs into a brief summary.

6.  Students continue to locate the magnet words from each successive paragraph and summarize, frequently using the magnet words throughout the text.

7.  Students become adept at noticing magnet words in paragraphs and no longer need to map them to determine if they are indeed supported. As they become more proficient at noticing magnet words, students begin to summarize the text naturally while they read.

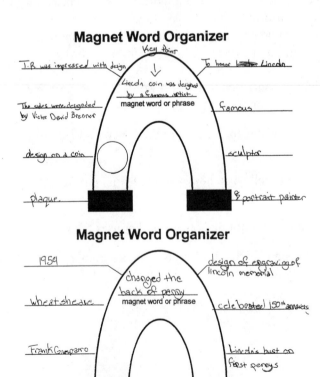

**Magnet Word Organizer**

**Magnet Word Organizer**

# Magnet Word
## Summary Sheet

| | |
|---|---|
| Lincoln coin was designed by a famous artist<br><br>1 | Changed the back of the penny<br><br>2 |
| George Washington helped make the first silver coins<br><br>3 | <br><br>4 |

The front of the Lincoln coin was designed by a famous artist. Fifty years later the back of the penny was changed to the Lincoln Memorial. George Washington helped make the first silver coins.

# Magnet Activity

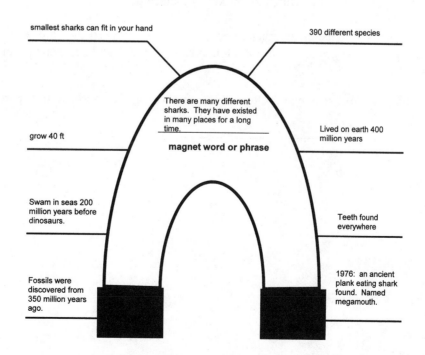

smallest sharks can fit in your hand

390 different species

There are many different sharks. They have existed in many places for a long time.

**magnet word or phrase**

grow 40 ft

Lived on earth 400 million years

Swam in seas 200 million years before dinosaurs.

Teeth found everywhere

Fossils were discovered from 350 million years ago.

1976: an ancient plank eating shark found. Named megamouth.

## Nonfiction Retelling

Summarizing or retelling of nonfiction text requires additional considerations from the reader. Nonfiction text places different demands on the reader than narrative text. In nonfiction text, the reader must flush out meaning in order to retain and use the information. Attention must be paid to the author's intent. Nonfiction text does not offer the same latitude of interpretation as fictional text. Retelling activities with nonfiction text focuses the reader on organization, vocabulary and concepts while they are reading. A retelling of nonfiction text includes the written text as well as the information housed in the graphics and illustrations.

Fluent nonfiction readers search for concept development while they are reading creating greater understanding at the completion of the text. Marking text is another activity that boosts students' comprehension by focusing their reading on what is worth learning and remembering. Pausing to make notations in text helps students' assess their comprehension by making them aware of what they are doing and not doing to promote comprehension.

## Textual Highlighting Technique

Distribute blank overhead transparency film and marker to each student.

1. Instruct students to place the overhead transparency over the text they are reading and mark with highlighting pens any important information, notable features and additional information they want to remember.

2. After reading the text, use the highlighted information on the overhead transparencies to summarize the text.

## TEXTUAL CODING SYSTEM

Create with the class an agreed upon set of coding systems for monitoring and promoting comprehension while reading nonfiction text. The following is a list of suggested codes:

I — for interesting
C — for connection
* — for important
N — for new information

? — for question or need for further inquiry
A — for agree
D — for disagree

*Note: The ideas and activities presented to this point work extremely well in whole group settings used during shared reading techniques. In order for the teacher to monitor students' strengths and weaknesses while reading nonfiction text, a more in-depth look is needed. At regular intervals, students need to meet with the teacher in smaller groups, investigating and reading nonfiction text that matches the students' instructional reading level. Students need to read material they are comfortable with while they fine-tune their nonfiction reading skills in this small group setting.*

## NONFICTION GUIDED READING

In a small group setting, with multiple copies of a piece of nonfiction text at the students' instructional reading level, have students articulate their thought processes while reading the text. Focus the discussion not on what was read, but how it was read and why it was read in that fashion. Prompt students to consider the following while reading:

**General questions**—These types of questions alert children to the more complex challenges of nonfiction text.

- How would the amount, authenticity and presentation style of the information affect the rate of reading?
- How might other nonfiction authors approach the same topic or theme?
- What impact does the illustrative style have on the information presented?
- How is the text crafted?
- What information should be selected and shared with others?

**Questions Prior to Reading**—These queries are designed to demonstrate for children how to read beyond the superficial, assuming control for considering, evaluating and applying what they have read.

- How do you think the author will treat this topic?

- What other texts have you read by this author? What style of text are you expecting to read?

- What comments do you have about this author's style?

- What expectations of the book did you get from the cover?

- What clues do you get from the table of contents or chapter heading?

**Questions During the Reading**—These questions help students clarify, amend and confirm their purpose for reading and their expectations of the text.

- How does the text confirm, add to or change what you already know?

- Is the text confirming what you expected to find? Why or why not?

- How has this information added to your understanding of the topic?

- What are the key points the author is presenting?

**Questions for Rereading the Text**—These questions can encourage rereading with a specific or different purpose in mind.

- What do you think was the significance of _____?

- Which information is the most important? Why?

- What would you do if you were planning notes for an illustrator?

    (See Chapter Three for more on questioning.)

# In Conclusion

Nonfiction material is as diverse in structure and design as the topics it covers. Reading nonfiction material is a challenging and rewarding process. Teachers who foster the art of inquiry and discovery of nonfiction text in their classrooms also teach students to be adept readers on nonfiction material by providing extensive modeling and specific explicit instruction on how to read for information.

# Questioning Techniques

## Introduction

Examining a nonfiction topic in an inquiring way is an exciting, fulfilling type of reading, resulting in new insights, connections and understandings. Unfortunately, this involving experience is limited to students who are proficient in this style of reading. Intermediate students are eager readers of nonfiction, especially innovative texts, such as pop-up books, books with transparencies or cross-section overlays. Many strategic reading activities assist students in constructing meaning in these distinctive texts, but the use of questioning as an ongoing meaning-maker is one of the most productive activities for readers.

Teachers need to provide effective inquiry models for students but rarely does modeling alone turn a student into a proficient self-questioner. Additional in-depth instruction that supports and evaluates the students' ability to use questioning and responding techniques must occur before students naturally employ active questioning techniques on their own. Questions of substance come only from curious learners who know enough about a topic to ask thought-provoking questions. When students read text exploring a nonfiction topic, they are only able to ask questions about something familiar to them.

Prior to reading, teachers should create and establish background information for students in a variety of ways before students are asked to read in an inquiring way. The more students know about a topic, the more active questioning they use while reading, promoting full and deep understanding of text.

Considering that most reading is done as an individual act, students must be taught to construct meaning on their own, with a variety of texts. Setting the stage for reading by asking guiding questions about key concepts prior to reading is an excellent nonfiction technique. Self-questioning during reading to clarify and extend the meaning of text is critical for successful reading and interpretation of nonfiction material. Questioning done as a post-reading activity allows students to sort and classify information for retention. Students who actively promote further inquiry after they have carefully read the text and understand the concepts are building bridges between their prior knowledge and the new concepts and information they have received. This chapter examines the power of enabling students to be able to ask thoughtful questions throughout the entire process of reading nonfiction text.

## Modeling Questioning

Teachers need to promote and model questions in an environment of inquiry. A natural way to model ongoing questioning is to stop during a read-aloud passage and ask students questions such as: What do you think the author will tell us next in this piece? Where do you think the author got this information? What additional information do you want to know about what was just read? Another way to model effective questioning techniques is to ask a variety of questions while students are sharing information they have learned from reading nonfiction text. Pose such questions as: Did you learn as much as you thought you would while reading this book? Was there any information that surprised you or that you weren't sure was accurate? What did you do when the information presented seemed inaccurate? Encourage students to ask themselves and others these types of questions. Modeling, in conjunction with instruction and evaluation, provides students with reading behaviors they need when questioning for meaning. Try the following ideas to promote active questioning:

## QUESTIONING ALOUD

As the nonfiction text is being read aloud, stop and verbalize questions that come to mind as well as possible answers. Talk to the students about why readers ask themselves questions and how asking questions assists with the meaning of text. Invite students to join with you in this question-and-answer response. Possible questions are:

- Have you read or seen something like this before?

- What information do you already know that connects with what you are reading?

- Is there anything more you would like to know?

- What is the tone of the text?

- What is the author's point of view?

- How did the author get this information?

- Is the information accurate?

- Do you agree with the information presented?

- What information do the graphics tell you?

- Why did the author write this?

- How does this text make you feel?

- How do you visualize the topic or concepts in the text?

- Did you learn what you originally expected to learn?

- How did you decide which sections were most important to read?

- How do the captions and titles help you read this text?

- Did the organization of the text help you understand it better?

Encourage students to join in this shared questioning and ask a variety of questions. Provide students with a list of verbs that helps students' inquiry become more expansive. Possible verb choices are:

| | | |
|---|---|---|
| sequence | describe | identify |
| explain | illustrate | conclude |
| transfer | select | apply |
| differentiate | contrast | distinguish |
| analyze | organize | construct |
| judge | decide | appraise |
| assess | criticize | justify |
| evaluate | rank | conclude |

## CLASSROOM OR SCHOOLWIDE QUESTIONING

Locate a central spot in the classroom, library or school hallway and ask students to record and post in this spot any questions they have concerning nonfiction topics. Encourage anyone, including other students from different grade levels, teachers, school personnel, parents, etc., to read the questions and write down information related to the questions. This open exchange of information establishes a school learning community that seeks out and shares nonfiction material.

## NONFICTION QUESTIONING FORMAT EXPLORATION

Use nonfiction question books as models for divergent questioning formats. Collect as many questioning-style nonfiction books as possible. An excellent nonfiction book written in a questioning format is *Football Math*, written by Jack Long. Read as many questioning-style nonfiction books to students as possible and discuss the questioning format and methodology.

While examining these nonfiction texts, focus students' attention to the questions authors use to draw the reader's attention. Locate and share with students books, articles, magazines, etc., that use a questioning lead approach in writing.

## Read My Mind

Play Read My Mind with students to model basic questioning/thinking techniques. Think of a concept and topic familiar to students. Give students five clues, one by one, each time releasing more information about the topic. After each clue, have students guess what the topic or concept is. The object of the game is to guess the topic or concept using the fewest amount of clues.

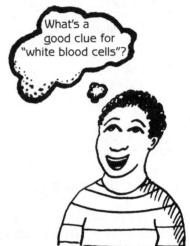

Example:    Concept being studied—circulatory system

Topic—white blood cells

Clue 1—This can be found in your body.

Clue 2—It travels in your circulatory system.

Clue 3—They number in the millions.

Clue 4—They are used to fight infection.

Clue 5—They are known by a certain color.

Once students have learned how to play the game with a teacher leader, they can play this game on their own. One student thinks of a piece of information or fact learned from a nonfiction text that they would like to share with the rest of the group. The selected student then thinks of several clues describing this piece of information. When the clues are prepared, this student states the clues one at a time, giving the group one chance to guess the concept or topic for each clue.

## Questioning Games

Have children practice thinking of questions that elicit a certain type of information. Playing the game Twenty Questions is an excellent way to begin this thought process. Think of a concept or topic that students have learned. Have the students ask up to twenty questions regarding the concept or topic that can only be answered by a yes or no response. Students quickly become adept at devising questions that provide them with as much information as possible. Spend time teaching students more elaborate questioning games such as Trivial Pursuit, Jeopardy, etc. Posting a daily riddle on the board in the morning is another way to keep students questioning and searching for answers.

## FIVE QUESTIONS

After students have been exposed to a variety of questions have them practice writing, sharing and evaluating questions in this short writing activity. Give students simple answers such as "gum," "blue," or "apples" and ask them to write five questions that could be answered with the single word answer. Share the questions with the rest of the class and discuss the quality and variety of created questions. Post the most interesting, unusual and thoughtful questions in the room for further reference.

# Questioning in the Beginning

Why does a student choose a piece of nonfiction text to read? What underlies the decision to seek out this particular text? Frequently a question, a wonderment or the ultimate query, curiosity, precedes the choice. Students need to be encouraged to actively research their interests and inquiries. The stunning amount of information available today requires an almost innate sense of discovery. Excellent questioning leads to partial answers and even greater questions. Viable classroom communities promote and value the act of inquiry.

Prior to a unit of study, it is common practice to generate and record student questions about a topic. This free flow of questions is an excellent way to stimulate thought. But what happens after the questions are generated? Do all the questions get answered? How does any one student find all the answers? Are all questions equally important? Current practice in questioning needs to move beyond the listing of random questions to provide students with a way to use the questions to focus their attention and guide their thoughts. Organizing ideas and thoughts before reading makes the reading process more efficient. Rather than just gleaning random bits and pieces of information from text, readers sort and select the information they want to gain from the reading experience.

## CONTENT AREA TEXTBOOK DISCOVERY

Use the textbook structure that bullets or bolds the important information as a tool to assist readers by having students change the bold print, captions or bullets into guiding questions. The student example shows how the student organized his inquiry by using the text structure as a guide.

After students have created their guiding questions, they may record these questions on the left of a piece of paper, leaving the right side for note taking, marking down insights or recording information that addresses each question.

*Textbook Discovery*

What does volcanic ash look like?

How are cinder cones formed?

How are shield volcanoes different from other volcanoes?

What are the characteristics of a composite volcano?

# Questioning During Reading

Deep comprehension and constructing the meaning of text relies on a reader's ability to take note of the type of questions proficient readers ask themselves about a text before, during or after reading. Students need to use questioning techniques to assist them in clarifying meaning throughout text. Along with using questioning techniques, students need to become familiar with many types of questions: those that the text answers specifically as well as those that the author implies. Most importantly, students need to learn how and why questions focus their reading of text, creating deeper and more meaningful comprehension.

The broad range, styles and formats of nonfiction text, coupled with the many reasons a reader chooses nonfiction text, creates a situation where one successful approach to promote active questioning is to teach students generic guiding questions that focus their inquiry.

## Cue Card Questioning

Give students cue cards listing generic questions. Students store these questions in their desks and at home to use as guidelines when reading nonfiction text. Sample questions are:

- How are _____ and _____ the same?
- How are _____ and _____ different?
- How did _____ affect _____?
- How did _____ cause _____?
- Why did _____ happen before _____?
- What will happen if _____ does _____?
- What if _____ did _____?

## Author's Quest

Another interesting way to read, remember and reuse nonfiction material is to use the author's point of view as a catalyst. Tell students to imagine they are working alongside the author as the text is being written. As they read, have students write down the questions they think the author was trying to answer. Leave the list with the book so other students can use the questions to focus their reading. Students can continue to add to this list of "author's" questions.

Sample questions:

- ▢ What does the reader already know?

- ▢ How much more do I need to tell the reader here?

- ▢ Should I change the title to _____?

## QUESTION CHART

| WHO | |
|---|---|
| Q. | _____ |
| A. | _____ |
| Q. | _____ |
| A. | _____ |

| WHEN | |
|---|---|
| Q. | _____ |
| A. | _____ |
| Q. | _____ |
| A. | _____ |

| WHAT | |
|---|---|
| Q. | _____ |
| A. | _____ |
| Q. | _____ |
| A. | _____ |

| HOW | |
|---|---|
| Q. | _____ |
| A. | _____ |
| Q. | _____ |
| A. | _____ |

| WHERE | |
|---|---|
| Q. | _____ |
| A. | _____ |
| Q. | _____ |
| A. | _____ |

| WHY | |
|---|---|
| Q. | _____ |
| A. | _____ |
| Q. | _____ |
| A. | _____ |

Have students create and record their questions and predicted answers about a topic prior to and during reading using the Question Chart as an organizer. The questions students create should encompass ideas they found interesting and want to know more about, as well as ideas brought on by the title, graphics, etc. The basic question word-structure assists students by focusing inquiry, while activating and assimilating prior knowledge.

For example, while reading an article about the national landmark, Ellis Island, the following questions are generated.

- ❓ Who paid for the rebuilding of Ellis Island?

- ❓ Who finally decided to close Ellis Island as an immigration site?

- ❓ Who were the people who processed the paperwork admitting the immigrants to this country?

After students have focused their attention by recording a variety of questions, they write predicted answers for the questions. To answer the question "Who were the people who processed the paperwork admitting the immigrants?", students need to draw upon their knowledge of the time period, including the customs and cultures of all economic levels in society. Students need to sort through information they know about the governmental practices and policies of the time period. Students also need to recall other information they have read or heard about immigration at Ellis Island. Based on the information they have, students may record several answers to this question. A possible answer might be all male governmental employees. Another possibility could be women as well as men governmental employees. Students may consider volunteer organizations such as the Red Cross. Still other possibilities might include the law enforcement agencies. Once these preliminary answers have been established, students actively read, searching to confirm or adjust their predicted responses. The students have created a compelling reason to read; confirmation of their assumptions. Another reason for reading is the search to find answers for questions that interested them but they could not answer on their own. Predicting preliminary answers for questions engages the student by accessing the students' own resources, background knowledge and experience before reading and interpreting text.

Ask students to read nonfiction text, keeping the question chart on hand. Have them change their predicted answers whenever the text reveals information that adds to their understanding and changes their responses, even slightly. When students are finished reading, have them underline, circle or highlight answers they now consider correct. They can pursue other related texts to seek additional information.

## QUESTION, INFER, RESPOND

While working in pairs, direct students to read several sections of text. (The text may be divided up by paragraphs, columns or pages.) After reading each section, students take turns generating a question to ask their partner. The questions students ask each other should require thinking beyond the text. The questions may ask the respondent to analyze the author's textual information and apply that information to another situation or topic, as well as infer beyond the literal level. For example, in a nonfiction piece describing the intelligence of dolphins, the question, "How could the author's examples of dolphin intelligence be applied to other animals?", will require critical thinking skills to answer appropriately.

The students then ask their partners the questions they have generated. Together in pairs they evaluate and discuss the responses. Due to the inferential nature of the questions, much discussion occurs frequently requiring that students go back and reread the text or consult other sources. When the complete text has been read, the whole group comes together for further discussion.

One of the most effective ways to construct and absorb the meaning of text is to connect known information to the new. One of the most extensive areas of research in reading has been done in the area of schema theory, which explains how learners store their knowledge and are able to remember what they have learned. Accessing background information is a common tool used to assist meaning making in nonfiction text.

## MAKING CONNECTIONS

When students are reading and encounter new textual information or key concepts, have them make connections with this information on three levels: connecting text to their personal experiences, connecting text to general background information they have learned or connecting text to other related materials they have seen, heard or read.

The following example is a bookmark placed alongside the students' text while reading. While students read the text they jot down information in the appropriate location of the bookmarking sheet. After reading, use the students' connection sheets for small group discussions. Students share the key information they selected as well as the connections they made while engaged in the constructing meaning process.

### Making Connections

Answer the following questions after you have read _____.
(Text means what you have read.)

How does the text relate to your life? _____

_____

How does this text relate to something you heard about?

_____

_____

What other information have you read about that helps you understand this piece of text?

_____

_____

# Questioning After Reading

Reflection after reading provides the opportunity for students to deeply process important information or create conditions for further inquiry or discussion. More time is available to consider, sort, organize and respond to thinking generated by a piece of nonfiction text. Often these types of post-reading questioning activities are done as a whole group in the intermediate classroom. Consider alternate grouping options that actively involve students in this meaning-making process.

## 3D QUESTION SORT

Content area textbooks include questions at intervals throughout the chapters. After reading a section of text have students copy the questions from the text and sort these questions into three categories, define, detect, and decide. The three categories reflect the thought processes needed to determine the answer for the question. Definition questions are those where the answer is clearly stated in the text. Detection questions differ from definition questions as the answer is determined by using textual clues, and decision questions are answered by using personal choice and experience.

After students have designated a category for each published question, they evaluate the range of questions represented in the text. If the published questions are primarily in the define category, students can create additional questions that span all three levels of questioning.

Once students are familiar with these three categories of answer responses, they can evaluate their own questioning techniques by judging whether or not the questions they create span this range from defining to deciding.

## QUESTION CHAINS

Successful readers are often intrigued and challenged when they hear questions other readers have considered while reading nonfiction text. Hearing the inquiry of others often inspires the reader to think of new questions. Question chains allow all students to practice this type of question generalization. In small groups, one student poses a pertinent question concerning a piece of nonfiction text, and rather than answering the question, other students in the group take turns asking questions related to the first question posed. These string of questions are then recorded on long strips of paper around the room, focusing inquiry and sparking deeper and more diverse comprehension of text.

Once the chains are complete, students reread the text looking for answers to the numerous and diverse questions on the questions chains.

Once students have experienced a vast array of various questioning styles and techniques, they begin to see the correlation between questioning and constructing meaning. The bridge has been built between simply being able to construct a good question and the ability to use a question to enhance comprehension. The following activities are excellent ways to assist students in evaluating the types of questions that successfully promote understanding.

## TEN QUESTIONS

While introducing the students to a new topic of study in nonfiction text, have each student write down ten questions suggested by the topic. After reading the text, each student writes ten more questions that are needed to clarify text, extend text or enrich text. Each student compares the two lists of questions to determine how they were the same or different, which questions were the best and why and which questions were the easiest to write and why. The same procedure can be done using the illustrations and graphics found in nonfiction text.

## IMPORTANT QUESTIONS

On a weekly basis have students create and record their questions concerning the nonfiction texts they are reading. Next to the question, have the students record why the question was important for them to ask. At the end of the week, each student chooses one question to read to the group. The rest of the students listen to the question and speculate why the author of the question felt it was important. At the end of the discussion, the author of the question reveals why the question was important for them in their reading.

Students at the intermediate level often choose nonfiction text for their independent reading. When students are reading independently in the classroom, as in a Reader's Workshop setting, provide interesting and thought-provoking questions for students to consider and offer a response. This type of question modeling broadens the students' own repertoire of questions by promoting thoughtful and diverse reader's responses.

## NONFICTION READER'S WORKSHOP RESPONSES

The following questions provide a wide range of questions for nonfiction independent response:

- Is the text worth recommending? Why?

- Are there things that you read that you already knew?

- What new things did you learn from reading this text?

- Can you visualize the topic in the text?

- How did the author bring the readers into the text?

- What is your opinion of this topic? Does it match the author's opinion?

- Compare this text with other information you've heard on the topic.

- Did the illustrations go along with the content of the text?

- How did you decide which sections were most important to read?

- What was the author's opinion/or point of view?

- What is the tone of the text/the author's point of view?

- How did the author get his information?

- ▣ Why did the author write this?

- ▣ What would you ask the author about the topic?

- ▣ If you were present at the time, how would you feel?

- ▣ What came as a surprise to you?

After students have responded in writing to a question, groups of students who answered the same questions may join together for a brief discussion. This promotes a lively discussion of nonfiction and the special attributes and challenges it offers.

## In Conclusion

Proficient readers spontaneously ask and respond to questions throughout the reading experience. These questions are not always based on the explicit information in the text but extend beyond into author's intent and reader's interpretation. Proficient readers recognize that the art of questioning focuses their reading efforts and provides them with richer, deeper reading experiences.

# Implementing Graphic Organizers

## Introduction

The brain functions as an organizational machine. It is an information-seeking device, continuously sorting and classifying input. When receiving data, the brain actively searches for patterns or systems and in the absence of such organization, creates it. An effective method for processing the enormous amount of information in nonfiction texts is to use some sort of graphic organizational device prior to, during or immediately following reading. When students have developed a repertoire of strategic methods for interacting with text, they can select the best organizer for the material being read, as well as the best method for their own unique style of learning.

When students are faced with numerous types, styles and dimensions of nonfiction text, they need to learn how to strategically record and remember the information they are seeking. An initial step when searching for important textual information is to determine whether or not this text supplies the type of information required. Many students, while in the mode of research, search out or retrieve from the computer all types of nonfiction material related to their topic. Narrowing the amount of materials by determining the most helpful sources is an important nonfiction usage strategy.

Once nonfiction resources have been selected, creating and using a recording method, a storage device for information, is a technique students need to learn to be efficient nonfiction readers. An eclectic group of students arrives for instruction in classrooms every year and each practices and prefers a unique style of learning. They need to be introduced to many varied, nonfiction organizational skills so that they may choose the approach most suited for them and learn it so well that it becomes a way of thinking. Students become enthusiastic readers of nonfiction when taught effective attitudes, routines and habits that guide their discovery in nonfiction text.

There are four types of organizing guides for nonfiction text: comprehension guides, concept guides, structure guides and prediction guides. Each type of organizational category assists students by giving them a structured format. This format directs students through the nonfiction reading process by emphasizing the organizational pattern, key ideas, key concepts, details, literal and inferential meaning, as well as the application of information.

## Comprehension Guides

The following guiding activities increase students' comprehension of text by focusing on the key ideas and themes in a piece of nonfiction text.

## WHAT AND WHY CHART

To boost thoughtful reading of nonfiction text, ask the students to use a chart format and record actual textual information on the left side on the chart, labeled WHAT. On the right side of the chart, labeled WHY, have students reflect on why this information is important to them.

## INFERENTIAL SKETCHING

This technique uses a pictorial rather than written technique to record and remember the overlying message or important information from text. In this instructional strategy, students are grouped with other readers who have read the same nonfiction text. Each student independently sketches the concept, idea or information most important to remember. Next students form a circle and one student displays his work. The remaining students in the group take turns stating what important information they believe the sketch is portraying. Only when all of the group members have shared their impressions does the student who created the sketch explain what he was representing.

As the students share their sketches, many main themes arise in the sketches, reminding students that not all readers interpret, learn or remember the same information. These sketches can be categorized, providing students with a pictorial representation of the main concepts.

## BALLOON ORGANIZER

This graphic organizer provides the student with an organized way to search for the key ideas as well as how the author provides support for the key points.

1. Students identify a key concept from the nonfiction text.

2. Using the balloon organizer, students record the key concept in the largest balloon shape at the top of the page.

3. Students record the subsequent supporting details, examples and explanation of the concepts in mid-size balloons.

4. Any further elaboration of the concept is recorded in the small balloons.

5. As an option, after students have flushed out the key ideas and supporting details, they may use the balloon organizer to rewrite the information in their own words, creating a retelling of the information in the text.

## Balloon Organizer

## CREATING VISUAL INFORMATION

When students analyze written text for its informational aspects, a pathway to retention and application is through the creation of visual graphic information to accompany the existing nonfiction text. Students decide which pieces of information need to be enhanced, or are representative of the key ideas and concepts of a text. Once they have determined what needs visual representation, have them choose from the following list of options to create their own visual graphic.

- Diagrams
- Picture glossaries
- Cutaway illustrations
- Cross-sections
- Flow charts

- Bar, column, circle and line graphs
- Maps
- Tables and charts
- Timelines
- Illustrations drawn to scale

# Concept Guides

Concept guides focus the attention of the students on individual ideas or concepts in the text. These guides help students with unfamiliar vocabulary words and the concepts they represent, as well as the multiple tidbits of information that can be found in nonfiction text.

## VOCABULARY ANALYSIS AND APPLICATION

This guiding strategy teaches students not only to notice and examine unfamiliar vocabulary, but also the critical thinking skills involved in acquiring new vocabulary words into the student's own language base.

1. Have students identify unknown words and evaluate their importance relevant to the key concepts in the text.

2. For each selected vocabulary word, students record in their own words what the "fact" or information means.

3. Next to this description of the word, students record the actual textual context of the word for future reference.

4. The last notation on each student's sheet is an explanation of how the student might use the word in the future.

# Vocabulary Analysis Application

| Word | Meaning | Text | Use |
|------|---------|------|-----|
| Specialist | people who work chiefly in one subject area | Historians today must know how to select the information they need from a huge number of facts. This is one reason they become specialists. | I can use this anytime I think of people who do a certain job. |
|  |  |  |  |
|  |  |  |  |
|  |  |  |  |
|  |  |  |  |

## PICTURE ASSOCIATION

After students read nonfiction text, have them create a list of all the key concepts they can remember. Categorize these concepts. Create a pictorial association for each category. For example, if studying historical events, the geography (represented pictorially with a map), the people (represented by a single person statue) and the industry (represented by a factory building) may represent the categorized concepts. The students then organize the list of key concepts under the appropriate pictorial headings.

## DATA BANKS

Another technique involving identifying key concepts and creating a graphic guiding system is the idea of data banks. Students can create their own data bank or use a data bank that has already been constructed to organize the key concepts in nonfiction text.

After reading a piece of nonfiction text, use a blank spreadsheet or chart and have students determine what categories of data they wish to collect. As the students reread the text, have them collect and record data in its proper location in the data bank. This technique involves identifying key concepts and creating a graphic guiding system.

## CONSTELLATION GRAPHICS

Give students a sheet with the diagram of a major constellation such as the Big Dipper or Orion's Belt. Have students write key concepts from text on each star in the constellation. The constellation graphic becomes a visual representation to aid students' memory for text.

# Structure Guides

Successful nonfiction readers approach text in a predetermined way, instantly organize their approach for recognizing and retaining information while they are reading. Identifying and utilizing text structure is one of the most important variables in the comprehension of nonfiction text. Reading for information is ineffective if readers can't identify and synthesize important and useful information. Students need to be sensitive to the organization of ideas in text so that they remember the gist of the piece, instead of random ideas and details. Recognizing text structure facilitates the chunking of information and the distinguishing of main ideas. Text structure schemata assist the recall of information from memory by providing a means of retrieval for the memory. Nonfiction text offers many organizational structures. These structures are evident in textbooks as well as trade books. It is the knowledge of these text structures that helps students organize an approach for nonfiction.

## NONFICTION TEXT STRUCTURE GRAPHICS

The following graphic organizers provide students with visual frameworks for recognizing how information is presented in nonfiction text. Students use the text structure templates to record important information according to the way the text was structured.

1. Locate, for the purpose of modeling, nonfiction text at the students' reading level, which is clearly organized into one of the following eight structures: definition/example, timeline/chronology, description, cause and effect, enumeration, compare/contrast, question/answer and problem/solution.

2. Distribute the appropriate organizer to students with a copy of the text. As a group, read and record the important information presented in the text on the text structure sheet. Note the types of transition words and devices the author uses to help structure the text. These provide signposts for the various forms of text structures. For example:

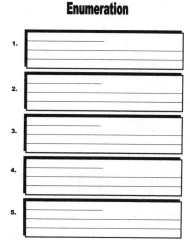

- Enumeration text structures use key words such as *first, then, finally,* and *before* in creating this structural pattern.

- Timeline/Chronology text structures use key words such, *"at the beginning of the new century"* or *"the next day."*

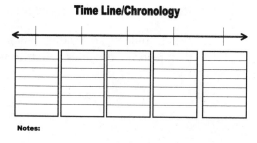

- Cause and Effect text structures use key words such as *because, so thus, consequently, as a result of,* and so on.

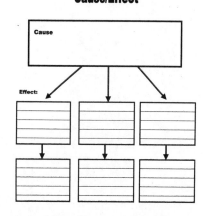

**Compare/Contrast**

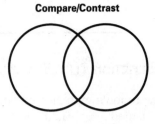

- Compare/contrast text structures use key words such as *by comparison, similarly, on the other hand,* and *unlike*.

**Definition/Example**

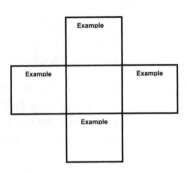

- Definition/examples text structures use key words such as *for example, such as, to illustrate,* and *namely*.

**Question/Answer or Problem/Solution**

- Question/Answer and Problem/Solution use a variety of transitional devices.

3. Repeat the modeling procedure for all eight types of structures. (See page 14 in Chapter Two.)

4. When students are reading independently, encourage them to identify the structure of the text and then record their notes and information according to the structure of the text.

# Prediction Guides

## PREDICTING AND CONFIRMING GUIDE

1. Students preview the selection and predict key concepts they expect the author to explain or elaborate.

2. Students write these concepts into four or five statements and record them on the predicting and confirming guide.

3. Prior to reading, have students write an additional sentence elaborating on the information they expect to read in the nonfiction selection.

4. During and after reading the nonfiction selection, have students record the concepts and any supporting information that the author actually included in the piece of nonfiction writing.

## INFORMATIONAL SQUARE

1. Students preview the text.

2. Using a square divided into nine equal boxes, have students predict nine pieces of information they expect to read about in this nonfiction text.

3. As students read, have them mark or color in the boxes containing information they accurately predicted would be in the text.

4. After reading, change the remaining information in the unmarked boxes to reflect accurate information based on the reading of the text.

5. An option for this activity is for students to switch prediction squares with each other prior to reading the nonfiction selection. Students then complete the prediction square of another student.

# In Conclusion

Nonfiction text provides many and diverse opportunities to learn. As with any worthwhile learning experience, it takes time, effort and planning to make it successful. Modeling and using graphic guides in the classroom enables students to march into the wealth of nonfiction text armed with techniques and strategies to harvest their information.

# Extending Nonfiction: Arts and Multimedia

## Introduction

Students learn better when they are motivated and receive frequent positive feedback. This challenges teachers to try creative alternative instructional techniques in their classrooms. Unlike fictional text, most nonfiction text does not have interesting characters or story lines to engage readers. In order to interest students in this genre, classrooms can give students the chance to explore nonfiction text through the arts and technology.

## The Arts

### READERS' THEATER

Readers' theater is an oral presentation of text with more than one reader. Readers' theater motivates readers by providing a real purpose for oral reading and a better understanding of the text. It also incorporates the language of the text into the students' own language. Readers' theater provides an opportunity for students with different reading abilities to work together. Instead of students taking turns reading a portion of published text, students and teacher carefully study the text in order to decide how the text should be read aloud and shared.

The first step is for everyone to silently read the entire text. The next step is to look at the text for possible ways to read the text with different voices. Voicing decisions are those that determine how many voices are needed to read the text and what parts each person will read alone or together with other readers. The group makes all these decisions after discussing the text.

For example, these voicing decisions can be considered.

1.  Using different voices for emphasis. Two or three voices reading together will put emphasis on words of importance.

2.  Deciding if time or seasons play a part in the selection. Use of different voices can highlight the passing of time.

3.   Using different voices to show points of view.

4.   Looking carefully at transitional words for points to switch readers.

5.   Considering main ideas of paragraphs being read by more than one voice to give emphasis.

6.   Dividing words in a series, such as adjectives or lists, among readers.

7.   Using different voices with text that compares and contrasts.

8.   Using more voices to increase the sound.

9.   Using voice to determine gender of the part read.

10.   Determining the role of a narrator, especially when a line or lines are necessary for understanding and flow of the text.

11.   Using different voices for repetition or add a voice for each repetition.

In addition to these voicing decisions, decisions need to be made on the words, phrases or sentences to be deleted and words, phrases or sentences to be inserted. These decisions are made to allow the reading of the text by multiple readers to flow naturally. Lines may also be cut to be done as mime, gestures or stage directions by the readers.

It is important that students understand there is no right or wrong way to read a piece of text in a readers' theater approach. The decision-making process of how to use readers' theater with a text requires rereading, understanding of text structure, comprehension and cooperation. The decision, such as the number of readers as well as which paragraphs and/or sentences are read by whom, is part of creating a readers' theater script. The final script is the individual's or groups' interpretation and understanding of the text. Oral reading of the script promotes fluency and expressive reading skills.

Deciding how to share the reading of any text as readers' theater involves higher level thinking skills. In fact, it is very enlightening for students to make comparisons when the same text is assigned to different groups. Each group will come up with various twists for sharing the text in readers' theater style.

The following poem has been divided for a readers' theater script demonstrating different ways students can show their interpretation of text.

Voice 1 and 2: *Indian Summer,* by John Greenleaf Whittier

Voice 1: From gold

Voice 2: to gray

Voice 1: Our mild, sweet day

Voice 1 and 2: Of Indian summer fades too soon:

Voice 2: But tenderly

     Above the sea

Voice 1: Hangs, white and calm,

Voice 2: the hunter's moon.

Voice 1: In its pale fire

    The village spire

    Shows like the zodiac's spectral lance:

Voice 2: The painted walls

    Whereon it falls.

Voice 1 and 2: Transfigured stand in marble trance.

**OR**

Voice 1: *Indian Summe*r

Voice 2: From gold to gray

    Our mild, sweet day

Voice 1: Of Indian summer fades too soon;

Voice 2: But tenderly

Voice 1: Above the sea

Voice 1 and 2: Hangs, white and calm, the hunter's moon.

Voice 1: In its pale fire

    The village spire

Voice 2: Shows like the zodiac's spectral lance:

Voice 1: The painted walls

    Whereon it falls

Voice 2: Transfigured stand in marble trance.

Voice 1 and 2: by John Greenleaf Whittier

Readers' theater activities are more successful when the experience begins with a warm-up activity. Use poems for warm-up activities. Collect a variety of poems and choose alternate ways to divide the lines among readers. Begin by selecting a poem and modeling ideas for how to divide it into parts. Using student volunteers, read the poem in different ways. Have students experiment with the task of planning a poem script on their own or in small groups. This activity gives students the experience and confidence they need when challenging nonfiction text is introduced.

*Joyful Noises Poems for Two Voices* and *Big Talk: Poems for Four Voices* by Paul Fleischman are books with collections of poems written for two or four readers. Students can also use these poems for practicing readers' theater techniques before they start making their own scripts to read and share.

After several experiences with planning a readers' theater script with fiction and nonfiction poetry, the students can begin to look at other nonfiction texts. Planning a nonfiction text for readers' theater involves even more scrutiny of text. Model the process by using the suggested ideas listed on page 00 for voicing. For example, the following text has been written for readers' theater to show voicing decisions, deletions ( ), and insertions ^ of text. (The text was taken from *Progressive Course in Reading*, American Book Company, Chicago, 1899.)

Voice 1, 2, and 3: (On the) Fourth of July 1776

Voice 1: The streets of Philadelphia were full of people.

Voice 2: (All) ^We^ wished to know what the Congress would do with the Declaration of Independence.

Voice 3: It was agreed that the bell on the State House should ring just as soon as the Declaration was adopted.

Voice 2: ^ I saw^ The old bellman climb(ed) up into the steeple so as to be ready to ring ^ the bell^.

Voice 1: His little grandson stood below to tell him when to ring.

Voice 1, 2, and 3: (They) ^We^ waited a long time.

Voice 2: The old bellman was tired. (but at last his little grandson shouted)

Voice 4: Ring, Grandpa ring!

Voice 2: The old man took hold of the bell

Voice 1 and 3: and swung it with all of his might. Never before had it sounded so clear

Voice 1, 2 and 3: and loud.

Voice 3: The Liberty Bell carried the good news to ^all^ the people of Philadelphia.

Voice 1, 2, 3, and 4: (By them it was) We sent ^the news^ all over the land.

Voice 1: Bonfires were lighted

Voice 2: (and) guns were fired.

Voice 3: Old and young shouted for joy, because our country was (to be) free.

Voice 4: (And) This is why the Fourth of July is a holiday. On that day the Declaration of Independence was adopted.

Voice 1, 2 and 3: Each year (the people) ^ we^ remember the day and think of the joyous news which the Liberty Bell first told.

Finally, carefully reread the prepared script before it is shared as a readers' theater. During this practice run, have students listen for smooth transitions between readers, the addition or deletion of some words for fluency and overall expression. When the final script is shared each child can choose one item to identify themselves in the script. This item may be a nametag, a prop that represents their role or a simple costume like a hat. Of course these props are not necessary to make readers' theater successful.

## STORY DRAMA

Story drama is a way to explore and extend text. In story drama, creativity and imagination take the place of staging and props. The use of oral language skills, including the practice of vocabulary from the text, is reinforced throughout the drama. Story drama is an excellent listening and speaking activity. Students are listening to the story text being read and acting as an audience when others are speaking. They are speaking as they play roles, as well as answering and asking questions.

A reader, often the teacher, reads the text and stops at points in the text where students can make predictions and draw inferences about the text. Students and teachers create and assume roles that fit into the time period and/or location describing the text. For example, students might be reading or listening to informational text about world exploration, major battles, rain forests or the Gold Rush era. The students and teacher create character roles that present factual information from these settings or events.

Perhaps the text being read is about the Gettysburg Address. On the day of the Gettysburg Address, who were the people who might have heard Lincoln's speech? Shop owners, laundry workers, stable workers, railroad workers, children and seamstresses are all possibilities. In this setting and situation, each student creates an appropriate character for that setting and introduces his/her character to the group. Each student determines a name, age and occupation for their character. Additional information including mode of travel, where they live and whom they are traveling with may all be part of this introduction. Characters introduce themselves to a partner, then each member of the pair introduces the other to the rest of the group.

Each character is questioned by the teacher or other students about their role in the event or setting. The teacher asks open-ended questions to spark conversation and discussion. Possible questions are: What do you think…? How do you feel…? What would you do…? Why do you think…? Why would you…? If you could do…? Students use their knowledge of the text, content-related background information as well as personal experiences to answer the questions.

After the students and teacher have introduced their created character, but prior to the reading of the Gettysburg Address, the following sample questions are asked.

- Why are you here?

- Who came with you today?

- What do you expect to hear in Lincoln's speech?

- Why was it important for you to be here?

- What have you heard about the Civil war?

- What do you know about the Battle of Gettysburg?

- How would you describe the setting for this speech?

- What will make this day memorable for you?

- How do you feel about being at the site of the Battle of Gettysburg?

These questions create interest in the text. Students make predictions and become actively involved. The open-ended questions invite participation by students because all answers are possibilities and no answers are rejected. Students learn to be risk-takers and participate in the drama experience.

Additional questions can be asked after reading the text. Students use prior knowledge, text information, personal points of view and creativity to answer questions.

☒ How do you feel after the speech?

☒ What does "all men created equal" mean to you?

☒ Has this speech changed your thinking in any way? How?

☒ What was your personal impression of President Lincoln?

☒ What might you do differently when you return home?

☒ What part of the speech will you remember to tell your children and grandchildren?

☒ What one word in the speech will you ponder? Why?

☒ How would you describe the mood of the people listening to the speech?

When answering these questions, students in character relate the message of the Gettysburg Address. Points of view, feelings and emotions of the student-created characters are shared as well as content-related information. The students' responses show their understanding of the text.

Next, present students with a text-related problem to solve. This problem solving activity is done either as a whole group, small group or individually. In the example of the Gettysburg Address, students can solve a problem suggested by the nonfiction text. Another choice is to solve a problem related to a contemporary issue. For example, what can students do at their school to show they understand Lincoln's statement that "all men are created equal"? Sometimes a spontaneous problem surfaces during the discussions and questions. If this happens, the teacher may decide to continue with the planned problem or may solve the presented issue. It is best to work on solutions to problems that have application to students' lives.

Any suggestions for solving the problem are shared with the whole group. This leads to further discussion and application of the solution to real-life situations. During the drama experience, students practice problem-solving skills in a meaningful way. The application to daily living is an important component. Making connections with students' daily lives motivates participation.

During or following the drama experience students are asked to respond in written form. These written responses are the students' reflections about the nonfiction text. This writing often shows the points of view of the developed character or personal points of view by reflecting upon the experience, such as "hearing" the speech by Lincoln. In the Gettysburg address drama, students may also write from the point of view of Lincoln, stating how he felt as he struggled with the content of his speech or his feeling about the country and the war. Through this writing, students demonstrate an understanding of the nonfiction text, interpretation and application of the text. Written responses give students an opportunity to use the language of the text in another format. The possibilities of written extensions are limited only by one's imagination and the imagination of the students.

# Other Content Drama Ideas

- Battle of Bull Run
- Boston Tea Party
- Signing of the Constitution
- Industrial Revolution
- Westward Expansion

- Town Hall Meeting in any city or development
- Mayflower crossing
- Round table discussion for world conflicts
- Visitation to different regions of the world

## THE REUNION

After students have read a biography, journal account or autobiography have them come together for a "reunion" and share what has been learned about each person represented in the texts. Each student is responsible for researching and learning details about the person portrayed. Students come together for the "reunion" dressed as the person being studied. When students wear "costumes" to represent an individual, it helps them in the presentation of that character, making it more realistic. Invite other classes to participate by visiting with the celebrities and asking questions for a meaningful way of sharing.

## AUTHOR PERFORMANCE

Students select a favorite author of nonfiction and conduct an author study. The sharing of the information concerning the author research is presented by role-playing the author. The student can give a speech as the author or the student can be interviewed as the author.

## CREATE A SCENE OR RECREATE A PHOTO

After reading a text, students select an interesting scene in the nonfiction text and act it out or use their bodies to create a tableau or "living photo." By asking the students to add dialogue to the scene or a caption to the "photo" adds another dimension to the activity. Students show comprehension, interpretation and application of text, as well as a chance to use the language of the text in meaningful practice. This activity requires students to work together to recreate the positions of people or objects in the illustration found in the text.

## Art Across the Curriculum

Meet with the art specialist teacher and discuss shared curriculum. Together, talk about the pieces of nonfiction text used to supplement a topic, theme or unit of study. Art teachers are able to teach art concepts, such as color, texture and perspective in conjunction with many subject area topics and themes. Art teachers are often willing to do an extension activity with the piece of nonfiction text you are using in the classroom. For example when studying the ancient pyramids of Egypt, the art lesson is a study of hieroglyphics.

Art specialists have access to pictures of art that represent themes often used in the intermediate classroom, for example, survival, freedom, ecology, discrimination and so on. In addition, the students can read informational text about areas of art, artist, regional crafts and periods of art.

## Artist in Residence

You can enlist the expertise of an artist in residence to make connections with the nonfiction text you are using in the classroom. Researching the availability of an artist in your community is necessary, but is worth the effort. For example, if the illustrations in the nonfiction text are photographs, a photographer can present the craft to the students.

## Illustrator Study

Students often study favorite authors who write fiction and nonfiction literature. An illustrator study gives students the perspective of the illustrator whose job it is to express ideas, point of view and enhance the text. Students learn about the use of media, metaphors, design, color and so on. When students have this additional insight into the relationship of text and illustrations they become better "readers" of text. Sample questions students explore are: How did the illustrator elaborate the text? Could the text be understood without the illustrations? Why or why not? How would you have done the illustrations? Does the media of the illustrations help you understand the text better? Why or why not? Students begin to use the illustrations to make predictions, clarify, explain and motivate reading. This deepens their understanding and interpretation of nonfiction text.

## ADVERTISEMENTS

Students make an advertisement of a nonfiction book either through art, drama or video presentations. The information presented must be accurate, attractive and informative. In order to present any type of advertisement, the students must go back into the text and evaluate it for highlights and support for their opinions. Students will make choices as to what to present in the advertisement and format style.

## MUSIC ACROSS THE CURRICULUM

Students listen to and sing historical and regional music in conjunction with the nonfiction text being studied. Topics such as current issues, conservation and recycling have music written for school use. Music educators teach their curriculum with different pieces of music, offering classrooms the opportunity to make connections through the content of the musical piece. For example, songs such as "Dixie's Land" and "Battle Hymn of the Republic" were sung during the Civil War. "Yankee Doodle" was used in the American Revolution as well as in the Civil War. Medieval and Renaissance music is available to coordinate with the reading of informational text about that era of history. Regional music can be used to connect with a topic if no specific lyrics are available or appropriate. Try reading the lyrics as a choral reading or plan a readers' theater script (see page 43) with the lyrics.

Singing or listening to songs and music in connection with reading information about a time period or topic of study provides the students with connections. The universal messages of music, as well as the everlasting endurance of music over time, are best understood when connections are made with other learning.

## DRAMATIZED REPORTS

Students present reports on nonfiction topics through the use of drama rather than with written reports. The reports are done as a radio or television interview or play scripts. The reports are presented orally or written with dialogue between characters to convey the information to the listeners. For example, a report on the polio vaccine is done as a skit between a patient and a doctor. As the doctor gives the patient the vaccine, the patient questions the doctor about the vaccine. A news reporter could "interview" Jonas Salk in another example of this scenario. The questioning and answering technique presents the information. Reports written in poetic forms such as a cinquain or diamente can be shared through readers' theater or choral readings.

## CHARACTER CONNECTIONS

Many pieces of nonfiction text involve some characterization. For example, a story about the westward expansion involves historical characters such as Daniel Boone, but many other unnamed characters such as a mother, teacher, settler, storekeeper or neighbor are connected to that person and may not be mentioned in the text. Character connections is an activity that calls for creativity. Begin by introducing a person presented in the nonfiction text. Students take turns introducing a new character by connecting their character to the text personality and embellishing that connection. The use of creative connections and background information is encouraged. For example, one student might take the role of Daniel Boone's neighbor, "Nelly," remembering him playing in the woods in their backyard. Another student, "Ralph," remembers him being very kind to all the animals he encountered. Daniel's "great aunt" could recall helping in the delivery of baby Daniel and so on.

In some nonfiction text there are no characters. In this case, students need to think about the characters that might be in the background. For example, a text about the rain forest may not have human characters mentioned in the text. Begin this type of character connection by introducing a native, land developer or conservationist.

The object of character connectors is not accuracy, but rather for creativity and topic possibilities.

## GUIDED IMAGERY

(This activity requires some preparation.) After reading a nonfiction text, write a guided imagery script including the time, place, sounds, smells and emotions represented by the text. Pause throughout the reading of the script to give students a moment to create an image in their mind. (Once this activity is modeled, students are able to write these scripts unassisted.) After reading about the Roman Empire the students are guided back through time to create the setting, sounds, smells and emotions of that era. For example:

You are entering the age of the Roman Empire. How many years did you have to go back in time to arrive here? What modern conveniences did you have to give up when you went back to this time period? What was the hardest thing to leave behind, the easiest? In what city did you finally arrive? What do you see as you look around? What colors? What shapes? How would you describe the streets? How would you describe walking on them? What is happening out in the streets? Look to the left then to the right. What do you see? What do you hear? What do you smell? How would you describe the buildings? What do the people look like? Look at one person closely. Is the person a man, woman, boy or girl? How is that person dressed, what is that person holding in the right hand, what is on his feet, is the person wearing anything on his head, if so what is he wearing? Does he look friendly? When you speak, what do you say? Now travel out into the countryside. What mode of transportation will you use? Who is with you? What have you taken along with you out in the country? Why have you taken those items? Describe the countryside. What colors, shapes and textures do you see? As you look around, what is especially beautiful to you? Stoop and pick something up from the ground. Look at this object. What is it? What color is it? If it has color, is it dull or bright? How would you describe it? Where will you travel to next and why? What do you hope to see there? If you could travel forward in time to the 21st century what would you want to tell people about the Roman Empire? What artifact do you hope remains for people in the future to see?

### STORYTELLING

Students become engaged in the art of storytelling when the teacher first models the activity. Begin by telling students about childhood experiences, family traditions, family heirlooms, accounts of interesting experiences and friendships. Students begin to share their own experiences with each other and the class. Once this open-forum sharing begins, point out to students that they are storytellers.

Model telling a nonfiction text in storytelling fashion, rather than reading the text to the students. Then invite students to participate in nonfiction storytelling. A few storytelling tips are: read the text slowly, think through the text by putting pictures in your mind and reread the text many times prior to storytelling.

# Technology and the Internet

Technology is an integral part of our educational system. When related to the curriculum in an effective way, technology enhances classroom presentations of curriculum and motivates student participation and involvement. It expands the curriculum and engages the students in discovering and exploring new concepts. Teachers take on the role of a facilitator instead of the primary source of information.

However, it is important to balance the old and the new. The art of asking questions and reading books are still important in our classrooms. Students need to learn to speak, listen, read and write with and without technology.

The goal of technology is for students use the technology to enhance learning and produce authentic products. Rather than teaching students technological skills in isolation, have students use technology to learn skills while they are learning content and producing authentic products from nonfiction areas. These products show knowledge of the content as well as the use of technology. This use of technology makes learning meaningful while broadening the students' knowledge. Technology should be used when it is the best choice for the intended purpose. Remember to continually assess how technology is working in the classroom and make adjustments when needed.

There are many benefits of using the Internet and other aspects of technology in the classroom, such as supplementing, enriching and reinforcing lessons. The presentation of an illustration or graphic adds to the discussion of a topic or concept. These illustrations help students visualize the concept and information, holding their attention and helping them to take effective notes. The auditory mode of discussion is enhanced by the visual presentation, helping students with different learning styles. The Internet presentation shows the complexity of a topic.

Because of the abundance of Internet sites and technological products, the best products and sites need to be selected for classroom use.

- Evaluate all CD-ROMs, Internet Web sites and software for creativity.

- Look for well-organized presentations.

- Evaluate the visual attractiveness.

- Check for activities that are interactive, e.g., the learner discovers concepts, thinks critically and is engaged.

- Know if information provided is in addition to or confirms textbook information.

- Evaluate for appropriateness for classroom use.

- Check if new concepts connect with the curriculum.

- Select sites and products with knowledge of students' background knowledge. (In some cases, the information may be too basic and at other times the information might be beyond students' ability to make connections.)

*Note*—It is impossible to keep up with the Web sites that are available and appropriate for school use. Sites are constantly updating their information and changing locations. Share current sites with colleagues.

## ARCHIVES

Use computer technology to save written artifacts on disk to be used as models of writing. Some excellent pieces of nonfiction writing done by the students can be saved from one school year to the next to be used as models in mini lessons. Students can look up pieces of writing for models in different genres. The fact that these written pieces were done by other students is a valuable asset.

Also, disk archives can be used to store pictures taken with digital cameras. Pictures taken during a classroom science experiment or any other classroom activity can be stored for later observation, review and confirmation. Finished products of student artwork can be scanned or photographed and saved on disk for later use as models.

## CRITICAL DISCUSSIONS

Students can critique television programs, videos and Internet sites by discussing the format or structure, audience attractiveness, organization and style. Some examples of different formats or structures to observe in videos and Internet sites are: problem and solution, process, problem with no solution and narrative.

## MAKE COMPARISONS

Students can compare and contrast information on a nonfiction topic from different sites on the Internet by using a Venn diagram showing how these sites are the same and how they are different. Lists of pros and cons about each site are generated and compared. Information from Web sites are compared with information found in nonfiction literature books, again using a Venn Diagram.

## CLASS TRIPS

The Internet is used to bring all kinds of museums from around the world into the classroom. An Internet class trip to a museum can be used as an introduction prior to an actual visit, culminating activity after a visit or a vicarious visit. The museums available on the Internet include: space, art, science, history, sports and others. By connecting these Internet visits to nonfiction text, students have an additional resource to aid their understanding. This understanding is enhanced with pictures and information presented in other ways, giving students the chance to observe and read information another time.

A follow-up to an Internet class trip can be additional readings of nonfiction text, summaries, journal entries, illustrations, experiments, debates and discussions.

*Note*—Before visiting an Internet site, students should be involved in prediction activities. Predictions will motivate the students, assist them in locating important information and clarify the purpose for the visit.

## LEARNING SITES

Computers are learning centers. As part of the daily routine, students have access to the Web to learn a word for the day, find out what happened in history on that date, as well as weather and current events. Use the bookmark system provided by the computer's software to mark these sites for quick accessibility. For example, the following sites can be book-marked for daily access.

- This day in History is at http://www.historychannel.com/thisday/

- Cool Word of the Day is at http://www.edu.yorku.ca/wotd/

- Current events are found on cnn.com

## STUDENT LINKUPS

Students interested in connecting with other students in foreign countries can use the KidLink network to make these connections. The site is found at www.kidlink.org. Teachers can set up a KidChat bulletin board to communicate with other students to discuss certain topics. Global Schoolhouse at http://www.gsh.org and Internet School House at http://www.internetschoolhouse.com are also for classroom linkups. E-mail messages between classrooms in and out of the school give students authentic practice in written communication. Making connections with students around the world teaches students what they have in common with each other.

Use these connections to collaborate on a joint project, quiz each other or share information on a common topic of interest. For example, students from different locations around the world are collaborating on the study of medieval times, space exploration or environmental issues. Each class shares information they have gathered about a topic. This type of interactive activity holds students' attention by anticipating new information, providing different sources of information and offering interpersonal connections with peers.

## PUBLISHING

Student can publish their nonfiction writings on the Internet. The Internet audience is a motivating factor for students, making them want to communicate more effectively.

## ANNIVERSARIES OF EVENTS

On anniversaries of world events, have students search the Internet to locate information regarding how the day is celebrated. Dates such as the bombing of Pearl Harbor, signing of the Declaration of Independence, first shot of the Civil War on Fort Sumter and the disappearance of Amelia Earhart are examples of these types of remembrances. Use these anniversaries to connect with the reading of nonfiction text.

## SCANNERS

Scan important illustrations in nonfiction text and project them so all can see the illustrations. Use the illustrations to extend the text lesson and aid comprehension. (This illumination can also be done with an overhead transparency.) Scanned illustrations can be used for discussion of artistic value and importance to the extension of nonfiction text.

Scan nonfiction text and project it on a TV monitor to look at the writer's craft for a mini lesson in writing nonfiction. This enlarged projection helps all students to share in the reading of the text.

Students can use the scanner to get pictures and other graphics to put into reports or to send pictures and information to other students through linkups.

## SLIDE SHOW PRESENTATIONS

Students can use a slide show presentation to create a piece of nonfiction text. Rather than a how to or step-by-step written report, a presentation of a report is done as a slide show on the computer rather than a live demonstration. These projects require critical thinking, problem solving, research skills and creativity when working with the technology.

Hyperstudio is another example of a way to use technology to replace traditional written reports by producing a presentation using sound graphics and text.

## CONNECTIONS

Provide nonfiction text that connects with current events reported on the Internet. As students read the informational text, they follow along with the event as it is happening on the Internet. For example, students read about a space exploration, hurricanes, volcano eruptions, Iditarod Race, and so on while following the current event in progress. The updated information is compared with the information in the nonfiction text by charting the information. Divide a piece of paper down the middle. On the left side record the information from the text and on the right side of the paper enter the Internet information. Use these charts for discussion by comparing, correcting and updating text information. Identify "holes" in information provided by both sources and discuss the importance of that information in the understanding of the topic.

## ASK THE EXPERTS

People who are experts on a topic are available to students on the Internet. Have students develop probing questions to ask an expert before contacting them. Have the students use Internet capabilities to contact the experts and find answers to their questions. Have the students work collaboratively so that many different experts can be contacted and their information shared. The following web site puts you in touch with experts in a variety of fields: **http://www.Askanexpert.com/ask/anexpert/**

## DESIGN A WEB PAGE

Designing a Web page requires the students to confer on graphics, text, organization and presentation. Cooperative planning and decision making is required for this activity. The Web page may offer information about their school or individual classroom.

# In Conclusion

The use of the arts and multimedia to extend the comprehension of nonfiction text is limited only by one's imagination. Reading professional journals is a great source of information for keeping teachers abreast of all the new uses of technology and ideas to integrate the arts.

# Writing Responses to Nonfiction Text

## Introduction

Readers' responses to text are an expected and valued part of the reading experience. When readers respond, they show appreciation and understanding. They make connections and apply information they have read. Some responses may not always be observable or immediate. Those observable responses are an emotional reaction, artist work, oral presentation or written response. This chapter focuses on asking students to give written responses to nonfiction text.

Students respond in written form to nonfiction text in much the same way they respond to other genres. When writing a response to informational text, students reflect on what they have learned, question their learning and state opinions about a topic. The responses are not designed to test the students' understanding of the text but to deepen understanding of the text and support students' reading comprehension. In addition, these written responses give students the chance to explore and use the language of text in more authentic ways. This exploration helps students internalize new vocabulary, concepts and information presented by the text. Written responses are short in length, and they are more interesting and rewarding than looking words up in a dictionary and learning the definitions or producing a summary of the read text.

Written responses to informational text vary in format and genre. For example, responses can be letters, diary or journal entries, poetic, dialogue (as in an interview) or written in narrative. The format for presentation can be oral, dramatized, illustrated or written. Responses are prompted by the different perspectives, such as point of view, emotion, humor, evaluation and personal experience.

Written responses also vary in what is required of the students. There are written efferent responses or those that require the students to furnish facts and details to demonstrate comprehension of the text. Application of the content or a personal response to the information presented in text is an aesthetic response. Some responses are written for a single piece of nonfiction text (intratextual) or a response is given to two or more sources (intertextual). A balance of response types provides students with varied practice. When selecting a written response for nonfiction text, keep in mind what genre of response is most appropriate for the nonfiction text being used. For example, historical content works well for diary accounts and timelines, while scientific text works better using an observation journal or explanatory narrative. Many other genres of writing can be adapted to work with all kinds of nonfiction text.

The following are ideas and suggestions for written responses to nonfiction text. As in any good writing program, written responses should be modeled first. Many, if not all, of these responses may never go beyond the first draft stage. However, these pieces can be saved in a writing folder to be developed at a later time.

# Writing Activities

## SENTENCE STEMS

Students are given a sentence stem to begin their written response to nonfiction literature. The stem can be specific to the text, for example: If the rainforest…, I think President Lincoln…, Blood suckers…, My heart…, Whales are…, The desert…, Mummies… and so on. Sometimes the stems are more open-ended, such as: I wonder…, If…, Maybe I…, Would it be possible if…and so forth.

## LISTS

Listing is an excellent response to nonfiction. Lists can include facts, questions for the author, people to whom the student would recommend the text, important words, events and people and plans for applying the information learned in the text to their lives.

In addition, students prioritize each item on the list according to different criteria. These criteria include importance to the student personally, importance to the community, level of difficulty, time and so on.

## NEW AUDIENCE

Students rewrite a portion of nonfiction text for younger readers. This writing experience helps students develop and interpret their knowledge of the content presented in the original text. Problem-solving techniques are used when rewriting text including illustrations, synonyms and deletions.

## DOUBLE-ENTRY JOURNALS

Students look at the text prior to reading and select a word, sentence or phrase that interests them. For students who don't demonstrate an interest in the topic, direct them to select something that caught their attention. On the left side of the paper, the student writes this word or phrase. On the right side of the paper, the student writes down the definition and/or thoughts provoked by the word or phrase. For example, students write about feelings, prior experiences and connections to past learning. Students share responses in small groups. This activity celebrates individual differences because each word or phrase selected is as important as the next. The variety of words, phrases and sentences shared create interest in the text.

Another type of double-entry journal is the dialectical journal done after students have read the text. Students use the left side of the paper to write down a concept they do not understand. On the right side students write what they think it means. Again students share in small groups, discussing the concepts, checking the text for clarification and determining an explanation for the concept.

## OBSERVATIONAL LOG

An illustration in the nonfiction text can be used for an observation log. In this activity, students write a description of what is being observed in the illustration as though they were writing to someone who is not able to see the illustration. This writing is detailed and highly descriptive in nature and can include observations using all five senses.

If only one copy is available, the illustration can be viewed by making an overhead transparency or by using a scanner to project the image on a TV monitor. This illumination of the illustration gives equal access to all students.

## CRITIQUES

When writing a critique of nonfiction text, students can express their opinions about the text, illustrations, format and so on. Writing a critique requires that students support their opinions with examples from the text. This type of response encourages rereading and further investigation of the subject. Before writing, students need to select the audience for the critique. Is the critique intended for the public in general, a friend, the author, illustrator or publisher, or is it a reflection on their personal reading selections?

In addition, the students can critique the text to make recommendations for publication in other languages. Students give their opinions stating in which other language/s this text should be made available and why.

## DIALOGUE JOURNALS

This type of journal between student and teacher or two students gives practice in using the vocabulary of the text, a place to clarify information, question and state learned information. When students write to the teacher, they express what they have learned from reading nonfiction text as well as their questions about the subject. When the teacher responds, the student's questions are answered and the student is encouraged and challenged with a new thought or question. Sometimes, a teacher's response may suggest further readings. When student-to-student dialogue journals are used, students are encouraged to write about the topic read. They may wish to include their likes and dislikes but also ask questions of each other. When students exchange journals they respond to the journal entry as well as state their own thoughts. In both types of journals, the language and vocabulary of the nonfiction text is used over and over. This repetition helps students learn new words and concepts while practicing the skill of written communication.

Asking students to dialogue with their parents is another option. This gives students another audience for their writing and is an opportunity for parent involvement.

## INTERVIEW DIALOGUE

In this interview dialogue, students write questions for a nonfiction topic of study and then answer the questions with information learned through reading or listening to the text. An example of this type of interview might be an interview with a germ. The student generates questions to ask a germ and uses the information of the text to write the answers to the questions.

## CONVERSATIONS

This response involves a conversation between two people, places or things in a piece of nonfiction text. The response is written in such a way that the student is able to demonstrate knowledge of the subject. Some conversation might be between the heart and the stomach, the Battle of Gettysburg and Battle of Fort Sumter, photosynthesis and a leaf or a globe and a map. These conversations encourage a student to reread and evaluate the text using the content and vocabulary to produce a meaningful conversation.

## DECISION-MAKING PROCESS

After reading nonfiction text; the teacher poses a "yes" or "no" question to the students concerning the content of the text. The students respond by writing both a positive and negative statement for answering yes and repeat the process with statements for answering no. Finally, the students make their decision as to how they personally would answer the question and write support for that decision.

### Decision-Making Process

**Question:** Can humans learn about family life from a wolf pack?

**Yes:** Humans can learn about family life from a wolf pack because we each have a family made up of mothers, fathers brothers, sisters. Just like wolves we bring home food to our family we each have baby-sitter. They have a baby-sitter to keep the babies safe so they do not get eaten. We have them to watch the kids to make sure they don't get into trouble.

**No:**

Because they have to hunt for their food. Wolves don't teach us how to hunt with a gun. They have to make their own homes.

**My own decision:** Yes I think wolves can teach us about family. We are almost the same. Besides for fur and how many legs we walk on. That is what I think about humans and wolves family.

## THEMED SENTENCES

Starting with a prescribed topic word chosen by the teacher, each student writes two or three sentences using that word. The prescribed word is the main topic, theme, concept or important vocabulary word in the nonfiction text. For example, in a text about the Civil War, the theme "freedom" is used in every sentence written by the students. In a text about the Industrial Revolution, the word "machine" would be used. After writing the sentences, small groups study the sentences submitted to delete, order and reorder them to produce an interesting piece of collaborative writing. These sentences can be organized according to content and length, from simple to complex or in any creative way students wish to organize. Other options include fact and opinion, true and false, less descriptive to more descriptive and location of the word in the sentence. Each group may wish to share their sentence grouping in a choral reading.

### "Comet"

The comet flew by our house every might for the last few weeks.

"The comet is traveling a tremendous speeds and the atomosphere can't stop it," said the professor

I saw the comet blazing through the sky faster than the speed of light.

How could a comet look so small yet is so large?

The bright firey comet of gas fell from the sky, it left only a trail of light.

I watched as the comet flew by, lighting up the sky.

Wide eyed I watched the comet soar through the moonlit sky.

We ate popcorn while we watched the comet.

We arranged them by the place of the word comet in the sentence.

# Comet

Last year scientists found a small chance of a comet hitting the earth.

The Comet is on its way, but it might collide with Earth.

Across the heavens a comet flew with a steadfast pace and wandering direction.

The comet hurtled into the planet's surface, destroying everything.

If you have a comet for an imagination, God bless your heart!

Bad friends are like comets, they always seem to run away.

Lightning is like a comet, you never know when it will strike.

Life is like a comet because it goes by so fast.

The first four sentences are things that are realistic. The last four are metaphors (analogies).

## POINTS OF VIEW

This writing activity begins by asking the students to state an issue presented in the nonfiction text. In small groups, the students discuss the issue from different points of view. Following this interaction, students write about the issue discussing the topic from the point of view of two or three different people or groups. These points of views may be from people close to an issue and from others who may be less affected by the issue. The issue of slavery during and before the Civil War could be written about from the point of view of the slave, member of the Underground Railroad, President Lincoln, southern plantation owner, abolitionist and so on. A government leader, farmer, nurse or a military person would have different points of views about chemical warfare. These points of view might even come from personified characters. For example, a foot or eye might write about the heart's value and/or role in the body. This type of written discussion involves higher level thinking skills as students evaluate the issue from the different points of view.

## Different Points of View

### An underground railroad worker

    Today I helped three people get across the Ohio river to the Underground railroad. They told me that they have been traveling for 2 months straight. They only ate three times over that long period of time. After that I took them across the river. I helped them get cleaned up and get something to eat. Then I showed them to the Underground Railroad.

### An observer

    Today, I saw the saddest thing I had ever seen. It was a slave being hanged. His head fell over to the side as he was saying his prayers. After five minutes the slave catchers left. As I walked over to let his body down from the tree, I could see the rope turning red. Blood began to run down his body. I hurried over to let him down so his soul could rest in peace. I gave him a proper burriel.

### A slave

    Today I had to hide in a nice mans barn. That night I was almost caught by dogs but I jumped in a river and swam away and cept on going.

Samples of fifth grade students' writing as written.

## PROBLEM/SOLUTION

Students state a problem related to the nonfiction topic and write a solution to the problem. For example, the Battle of Gettysburg created the problems of gun smoke pollution, death and widespread destruction. The solution to the problem of smoke, death or destruction would be the students' response based upon their knowledge of the problem and the time period in history. Students solve problems in many diverse ways. Other examples of problems to consider might be a plant or animal becoming extinct or the civil rights movement not meeting the needs of all Americans, farm land being sold and used up for housing developments, westward movement taking land from the Indians and so on.

## FACT/RESPONSE

Students state a fact from the nonfiction text they have read or heard. Students then respond to this fact with their own personal views, opinions and thoughts about the fact.

Fact    Pawnee Indians built homes along the river.

Response    I think they were smart to build homes along the river because they could use the water to get fish for food. They could drink the water and use it to keep clean.

## RIDDLES

Using the facts presented in the piece of nonfiction text, the students write a riddle. Riddle writing involves careful planning by the students in order to give important facts without revealing the answer. Usually the first clue in the riddle is very broad and has multiple answers. As each clue is written, the possible answers narrow until the last clue almost gives the answer away.

## JACKDAW COLLECTION

(A Jackdaw is a small European crow known for picking up items and carrying them away.) A Jackdaw "collection" is a list of thoughts, phrases and ideas that represent the content of the nonfiction book. Actual items representing the text are also included in the "collection." This activity encourages rereading as students evaluate and decide what bits and pieces to collect. Inferences about the text are also used in this activity. For example, a Jackdaw "collection" about worms could include a list of facts about worms, illustrations (student or published), a vile of dirt, a leaf, a worm colony, graphs of worms counts after a rain, personal uses for worms and so on.

## TEST QUESTIONS

Students write different types of test questions based upon the nonfiction text read. The types of questions would include those questions where answers are stated directly in the text, questions where answers use clues throughout the text and questions with multiple answers. These questions reflect what students see as the most important facts and issues presented by the text. This often leads to a discussion of what makes a good question.

## Thumbs Up and Thumbs Down

Students divide their papers into two columns. Students list information from nonfiction text by stating the positive things learned about the topic under the Thumbs Up column. The negative information is listed under the Thumbs Down column. In this way, each student evaluates facts and concepts recorded in the text in this decision-making activity. This response works well with informational topics that present a problem or an issue.

## Situational Perspective

Using an illustration from nonfiction text, students take on the perspective of an object in the illustration. This might be the perspective of a human, animal or something from nature (tree, blade of grass and so on). From this perspective, the student writes about what they see, hear, smell and feel around them.

## What's the Big Idea

Students write a single statement about the major idea or concept in nonfiction text. This statement is a fact or concept that everyone should know and understand. When writing a summary, students learn to delete, condense and conjoin ideas in their own words. Setting a limit of twelve words or less to the summary statement makes students work carefully with words to express the best meaning.

## CONCEPT CHANGE

Students select one concept in the nonfiction text to change in some way. In this written response, students state the change and explain how the change affects the rest of the content of the text. For example, if slavery had not been an issue of the Civil War how might the war been fought differently? Or suppose the Roman Empire would have had airplanes, how would this affect the expansion of the Roman Empire, cultural advances or common lives of the people? The rain forest and everglades are not in danger of being destroyed but rather will be expanding. What will happen to the developments on land, people and animals?

## ACROSTIC POEM

One word is chosen as the main concept, theme or topic of nonfiction text and used to write an acrostic poem. The word is written vertically and each letter starts a word or phrase that tells about the content of the text.

## QUESTION ANSWERS

Students write answers for questions about information found in nonfiction text. As the question answers are shared the students must state the question in response. For example, a question answer is "Abraham Lincoln." The question response could be "Who was the sixteenth president?", or "Who was the president during the Civil War?"

## Hollywood Producer

Students pretend they are a movie producer and the nonfiction text has been recommended for a production as a movie/documentary. Students write reasons for accepting or rejecting the text as a movie or documentary. Students consider the appeal of the topic, sources of information needed, location of filming and so on in this written response.

## Tell It in a Graph

Once a nonfiction text has been read students formulate a question based on the information of the text. Then they pose questions in an interview to others. These answers are presented in an appropriate graph form: circle, bar, figure or line. A written and/or oral explanation of the graph is also presented.

## *Try These Additional Written Responses*

- Book reviews

- Letters to authors and illustrators

- Personal recommendations for a text

- Synopsis of a book

- Book jacket

- Sequel

- Persuasive writings

- Charts comparing and contrasting information from different texts

- Rewritten endings

- Time line for a historical book

- Editorials

- Questionnaires

- Slogans

- Songs or poetry

# Additional Responses Beyond Writing

Writing is not the only way in which students might respond to the genre of nonfiction. Music can be sung or read as a choral reading. Drama and art are also ways to respond and are addressed in Chapter Five of this book. "How-to" books can be used to build and create, with many different medians producing a craft, recipe or experiment. Performance of an experiment from a science text or a demonstration of a craft are also responses that would motivate students to read and enjoy nonfiction text.

# In Conclusion

In most instances, students are asked to respond to the entire content of the book, but students can also be encouraged to respond to different sections of nonfiction literature. For example, students can respond to a book's introduction or afterword. A response can be written about the additional resources listed at the end of the book, such as the glossary, recipe or list of additional resources. An emotional response toward the subject or content of the text is also a possibility. The audience for these responses is important for the students to consider. Students can decide if the audience should be the author, publisher, illustrator or even the editor. See Chapter Seven, page 84 for more about audiences for student writing.

Responses to nonfiction should be shared. Learning to share and communicate are important skills in this informational age. No one reader can read all the available information, so students need to learn and experience the value of sharing information. Through the sharing of different students' responses, students continue to hear the language of the text, variety of different thoughts and formats, author's voice and repetition of the content information. By varying the response settings through use of pairs, small groups, whole group and displays, students maintain a higher interest level in the sharing process.

# Writing Nonfiction

## Introduction

An assignment in nonfiction writing is often met with groans from students. Summaries, outlines, reports and research papers are the most common types of nonfiction in intermediate classrooms. Why do students groan when asked about writing nonfiction text? They say, "It's boring." "We have to summarize every page." "We outline every day in Science and Social Studies." "Our research papers have to be ____ pages long." "I can't think of anything to write about?" "It's too hard." While there is nothing wrong with summaries and outlines, teachers need to introduce students to a broader range of nonfiction writing.

Writing reports, research papers and news reporting have traditionally been labeled nonfiction writing, but nonfiction writing reaches far beyond these formats. Nonfiction writing can be as simple as the retelling of a day at work or play.

Reading and analyzing nonfiction literature are the best instructional techniques teachers have to help students become good nonfiction writers. Students cannot be expected to write nonfiction successfully if they have not heard, read and enjoyed the genre. Students learn to write nonfiction well when engaged and immersed in the genre. Nonfiction writing is greatly influenced by reading and listening to the genre. In order to write good nonfiction, students must read nonfiction. However, readers of nonfiction are not naturally successful writers of nonfiction. They need to be taught and provided time to practice writing nonfiction.

When nonfiction literature is shared as a model for writing, students explore the varied styles and formats used in nonfiction writing. However when using nonfiction literature as a writing model, it is important that students have already heard or read the text. In a familiar text, a mini lesson can point out and focus on the techniques used by the author because the content of the text has already been explored and enjoyed in its entirety. During modeling, students hear poetry, journals, riddles, biography and narrative nonfiction texts. Through these exposures students develop their own sense of voice, style and format. Mini lessons teaching leads, author's voice, interesting techniques, formats, choosing a topic, revision and style can draw students' attention to ways in which they can write nonfiction.

Student writing can also be used as a model of nonfiction text or for mini lessons. Save students' writing samples so that each year more sample texts are available to show students how to write nonfiction. Samples are easily stored on disk for retrieval.

This chapter is about nonfiction writing. The activities will help students learn how to gather information, record and present information in a variety of formats. Along with the more traditional nonfiction writing of reports, outlines, research papers and summaries, give students exposure to many formats of writing informational text to eliminate the groans in response to nonfiction writing.

When introducing students to the following ideas in nonfiction writing, it is important to model the process and formats. When students do their writing, you are encouraged to work on a piece of writing as well. When students and teachers write together, they can share their struggles, ideas and decisions.

# Writing Activities

### ALL DAY, EVERY DAY NONFICTION WRITING

In this introductory activity, students see how often they write nonfiction and how important nonfiction writing is in their lives. Begin by brainstorming a list of all the nonfiction writing done by the students. For example, writing down a phone message is writing in the nonfiction genre. Notes to a parent about going to a friend's house, grocery lists, guest lists, directions and assignments are all types of nonfiction writing. Essential elements of nonfiction writing are as true in these examples as in any research paper. The information must be accurate, complete, organized, meaningful and informative. Explore with the students what would happen to any one of the listed examples of nonfiction writing if one of the above mentioned elements were missing. The importance of accuracy, completeness, informativeness and meaningfulness is apparent to students. Organization is easily illustrated by showing a random grocery list. Take this list and organize it by category, such as fruits, vegetables, dairy, canned goods and paper products. In a list format, this particular nonfiction writing is much easier to read and use.

### DISPLAY SITE

Students are given an area of the classroom to display their work. Students are responsible for their site and can display any work assignments. Classmates write to each other commenting and responding to their peers' displays. These comments can include praise and questions about the display and are addressed to the student in charge of a particular display site. These written responses can be displayed as well or shared only with individual students.

> I like your fish book.
> You could exhibit this to
> new fisher-persons. They
> would learn a lot. I
> learned a lot. I hope
> you get A⁺!

In order to provide additional audiences for these written responses, students are asked to write to their classmate's parent, principal or the classroom teachers, commenting on a student's display site.

## GENRE SWITCH

A unique nonfiction assignment is a retelling of information read that is written in a different genre. Asking students to rewrite expository text into poetry, song or even a newspaper article will guarantee no plagiarism of the text. Songs, poetry and newspaper articles can also be rewritten as expository text. For example, select a poem, such as one of Shonto Begay's poems from *Navajo* and rewrite that poem into expository text. In order to switch the information and do it successfully, students must use higher level thinking skills that enhance the comprehension of the original text. Consider the following genre switch ideas for nonfiction text: first person narrative, letters, journal accounts, speeches, picture books, script for a radio or TV play, field guide, riddles, news reports, editorial and poetry.

> They stood in the middle of blue
> Watching for land.
> Bad smells from the ships below
> Of people, cargo, and food,
> Cold seawater of fish and
> Drowned sailors.
> 60 days at sail
> Land! Land ho! they shout
> Straining to see the land
> Thicker and thicker grows the
> horizon
> The iron anchor drops
> Tis America

Note: This genre switch was from narrative to poetry.

## ABC Format

The ABC format is its own unique genre for writing nonfiction material. There are many varieties of ABC books. For example, have students write a question for each letter of the alphabet. These questions can be based upon any nonfiction topic, theme or a specific text. (Perhaps the questions will go beyond the information given in a text and invite further exploration and reading.) Other ABC book ideas are: writing a new concept or vocabulary word for each letter of the alphabet, alliterative sentences or writing a summarizing statement using each letter.

## Homework Notebook

Students are assigned to write a short summary in a class homework notebook after each content area lesson. This summary relates to what happened during the class period and highlights important words. Samples of math problems, illustrations that explain an activity, unanswered questions to be explored, next day assignments and important points to be remembered are examples of what could be included in the daily entries. This notebook serves an important function in the classroom. When students return after an absence from school, they read the homework notebook and find information they have missed. The job of recording is rotated among the students.

## INTEREST DICTIONARY

Students create a dictionary around a hobby, favorite sport, theme or activity. Students begin by brainstorming words of interest that are related to their chosen theme. Words are entered in alphabetical order with pronunciation key, parts of speech, definition and the word used in a sentence. Illustrations can also be added.

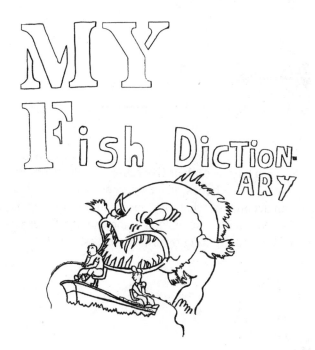

1.) barracuda. bar.ra.cu.da   bar'ə-koō'də
noun, fish of tropical sea.

I saw a barracuda when I Snorkeling in the ocean.

2.) butterfish. but.ter.fish   but'ēr-fish
noun, food fish found in the Atlantic.

Butterfish live in schools.

3.) Chinook. chi.nook   chi-nook'
noun, The largest Salmon.

Chinook salmon is such a beautiful fish.

## PICTURE REFLECTIONS

When doing a classroom activity in which students are participating, take pictures during the process. Ask students to reflect on the activity by writing what they were doing in each photograph and why they were doing it.

## OBSERVATIONAL ACCOUNTS

Give students the chance to observe the world around them through the use of their five senses. Students observe children at work or play, lunchtime activities, daily operations in the school's office or an activity on a street corner. After several minutes of observation, students write an account of what they observed through the use of their senses. Asking students to illustrate their observations adds another dimension to the activity, for example, constructing a graph, drawing a picture, recording a scene or highlighting one of the senses.

## SELF-REFLECTION OR EVALUATION

The heart of assessment is self-assessment, students writing an assessment of their own personal learning experiences. In this approach, students learn to critically evaluate themselves. This evaluation can be about a specific subject, single piece of work or a general evaluation of the learning process. For example, students evaluate a piece of writing or an entire writing folder. In subject areas, students reflect on what they have learned, need to learn or desire to learn in the future. These evaluations can be included as part of the reporting system to parents. Students are asked to write these evaluations with different audiences in mind; for example, the evaluation might be written to themselves, their parents and or teacher.

## Ponderings

Students write their theory about a phenomenon or event based on their knowledge of the subject after they ponder a puzzling scientific happening, current or historic event. Students include how this event might affect their community in areas of economy, jobs, safety and the future. For example, how does the United States space missions, new breakthroughs in medicine, World Series or famine in Africa affect them and their community? How is their future affected by the event? Will safety be an issue to consider because of the event and so on?

Dear Laura,

Today I saw my friend get killed. That's right he was shot to the ground. a guy got scared and he killed him. Why? Why did he have to do that? I'm glad I have a friend like you who would never do that. I wish my friend cuold hear this sound. You know what I hear? I hear the wounderful sound of children laughing, I love that sound. It is raining now. Wish you were here.

thanks for caring,

Tatty

Purple Flamingo

## Visualization

Direct the students to think of a personal setting, such as a bedroom, vacation spot, or favorite location and visualize that setting. Lead the students through a visualization process by directing them to "look" in different directions in their selected setting. Direct students to see the colors, arrangements and organization of objects in their setting. Direct students to special points of interest in their setting, asking the students to visualize deeply and think about special feelings they associate with this setting. Suggest an isolated spot in this setting where one might not be easily seen and ask students to think about how they are feeling; what comes to mind as they are sitting in this spot? What can be seen and heard from that vantage point? After the visualization experience, students write a descriptive piece about the setting they visualized.

## Write in all Areas of the Curriculum

Writing across the curriculum is one of the best ways to help students begin to focus on the topic of study. Ask students to write in mathematics, art, gym and other areas. Students use the language of the content subject and demonstrate their written literacy skills in that discipline.

For example, in mathematics students write math problems, interview a fraction or equation and explain how to solve a problem. In art, students write a self-evaluation of a finished product, title pieces of work, explain the process of an artistic work or describe an art lesson. In gym, students make up games and write the rules. They log, organize and display information on sporting events. In content areas, students write questions, summarize text and define vocabulary.

## Pre- And Post-Summaries

Students start the class with a written summary of the previous lesson. A brief writing session at the end of a lesson focuses on learning. Listing questions about the lesson presented that day provide a post-summary.

## Sentence Stem Summaries

Students complete the following sentence stems after reading or discussing nonfiction text: I feel... I learned... I wonder...

## RETELLINGS

A text retelling requires students' knowledge of the content and their command of the language to reconstruct the information of the text. After participating in the reading of nonfiction text, students can either work alone,

in pairs or small groups to write a retelling of the content of the text in their own words. The advantage of working in pairs or small groups is the discussion of the text along with the writing. The language of the text is practiced and used to construct meaning. With the original text out of sight, students discuss the content of the text, important vocabulary words, organization and format for retelling. For example, the text being retold may have been written in the format of a compare-and-contrast essay. During the group discussion this is noted and provides a framework for writing.

## LEARNING LOGS

Learning logs are a continual source of daily entries where students record what they have learned. In learning logs, students make predictions, ask questions and record thoughts and reactions to learning. To vary the activity, the learning log entry could be:

- a response to an open-ended question

- a list of important vocabulary words to learn

- a description of the learning process

- responses to a topic

- responses to individual learning

- statements of connections to previous learning

- predictions of future learning

- an illustration

- writing about how information will be used in the future

- points to discuss with classmates, parents or teacher

- connections with what has already been learned

- describing the learning process

- a statement of why certain information needs to be learned

## Questionnaires

After reading nonfiction text, students write probing questions about the topic. The developed questions need to allow for differing points of view. Using these questions, students design a questionnaire. Different formats for questionnaires include: yes and no, sliding scale (range of one to ten, agree to disagree), categories and short answer.

## Primary Sources

Primary sources are firsthand observations and thoughts in original form by the author of the text or illustration. Students are the primary source when they write about personal experiences, family, school and other memories. A journal entry, autobiography, letter, speech or illustration records the information.

## In Conclusion

Where does revision fit into these writing activities? Some of the activities such as display sites; observational accounts and homework notebooks are daily writings to demonstrate to the students the art of nonfiction writing. These are not usually revised. When written work is graded students should be given an opportunity to review the piece and make revisions. Activities such as genre-switch writing, ABC format books, retellings and writings done across the curriculum are excellent choices for revision and final copies.

Considering the audience for nonfiction writing is important when selecting the format for writing. The teacher is not the only audience. Students need to write to several audiences, including other students, parents, family members and governmental and agency members of the community. Authentic audiences are the most meaningful to the students.

Choosing the correct audience and the appropriate format offers a lesson in evaluation. When students are writing to the President of the United States in response to a text concerning foreign affairs, a business letter would be the appropriate format. If a student chooses to write a personal reflection on the same topic, a diary account would be appropriate. When students learn which formats of writing are appropriate depending upon the audience, they are evaluating the content of their writing and demonstrating comprehension of the topic and text. Along with the identification of authentic audiences, the sharing of student writing in the classroom is also important to consider. Schools need to teach students how to share their learning and insights. One way to share information is through student writing. When students elect to share their writing, the whole class celebrates their accomplishment. Students learn new points of view, review facts, hear the technical vocabulary and enjoy the styles of peer authors. Sharing like this is done in pairs, in small groups or whole groups.

# Assessing Nonfiction Use

## Introduction

The road to success in a world that revolves around the accumulation of information and knowledge is paved with nonfiction materials. The highway is broad and encompasses an overwhelming amount of nonfiction possibilities. Successful travelers are equipped with the knowledge of quality nonfiction materials; they know how to access the most valuable resources and read them productively.

Included in this chapter are many ideas for assessing and evaluating the level of students' proficiency when interacting with nonfiction text. The chapter concludes with ideas for judging how teachers and students have grown and developed as nonfiction users.

## Student Proficiency

Once a quality piece of nonfiction text has been selected and is in the process of being read by students, teachers need to use various instructional techniques to evaluate students' ability to confidently process informational text. Use the following ideas and activities described in previous chapters to evaluate students' ability to read nonfiction text effectively and efficiently.

- Graphic Examination Activity—page 11.
  This activity demonstrates whether or not students are accessing the graphic information in text, using the information as a preview, and setting purposes for reading.

- Nonfiction Predicting Arrow Activity—page 12.
  The text preview shows whether or not the student is using previewed information to organize and retain what is read.

- Text Preview Organizer—page 13.
  The text preview demonstrates whether the student is effectively using the signposts provided by nonfiction textbooks. The students' ability to preview the text and make accurate predictions of what information will be presented is evaluated.

- Text Impressions—page 15.
The summary of the text developed after reading using the text impressions word list gives teachers a way to evaluate whether students are able to use textual vocabulary appropriately as well as evaluate their ability to summarize major concepts and themes.

- Magnet Words—page 16.
The summaries created after the magnet words activity provide information regarding students' ability to find the author's key points and summarize major concepts and themes.

- Guided Reading—page 19.
This small group interview/observation process allows teachers to evaluate the students' use of strategies and techniques for processing nonfiction text.

- Question Chart— page 27.
This chart of questions and answers can be evaluated for students' ability to ask questions and predict possible answers that help guide their reading construct meaning at a higher level.

- Making Connections—page 29.
When students make meaningful connections to text, deeper comprehension occurs. This activity can be evaluated for the types of connections students are making with nonfiction text.

- Nonfiction Readers' Responses—page 31.
The nonfiction readers' responses are short answer essays regarding many aspects of nonfiction use. Evaluating these responses provides a vast array of information on students' comprehension skills.

- Balloon Organizer—page 35.
Students' ability to select key concepts and supporting ideas is evaluated in this graphic organizer.

- Creating Visual Information—page 36.
Creating visual information based on written text requires critical thinking to analyze significant textual information and recreate it in an alternate form. This activity allows students' to be evaluated not only on their ability to understand nonfiction text but also on their aptitude for critical thinking.

- Data Banks—page 38.
In this activity as in the previous activity, Creating Visual Information, the students' knowledge of text can be evaluated as well as critical thinking skills, which demonstrate if a child can analyze information, categorize the key components and recreate the data in an alternate format.

- Nonfiction Text Structure Graphics—page 39.
A key criterion for accessing information in nonfiction text is the ability to determine how the information is presented through the structure of the text. Using the text structure graphics indicates whether students are able to determine the organizational structure of the text and use that structure to organize information.

- Informational Square—page 41.
In this activity, students' ability to predict and then use nonfiction material to adjust predictions is evaluated.

# Effective Nonfiction Users

As students become frequent and fluid readers of quality nonfiction, they recognize accomplished authors of this genre. The more proficient readers of nonfiction text set quality criteria for the authors they select and use the same criteria to judge others.

## Authors' Features Analysis

Use a features analysis format to analyze the qualities of authors. Possible features to analyze:

Experience          Style          Voice          Clear Language          Humor

| Author | Experience | Style | Voice | Clear Language | Humor |
|--------|-----------|-------|-------|----------------|-------|
|        |           |       |       |                |       |
|        |           |       |       |                |       |
|        |           |       |       |                |       |
|        |           |       |       |                |       |
|        |           |       |       |                |       |

## Inquiry Observation

The reading and use of nonfiction material is dependent on the students' ability to organize for inquiry and be able to locate required information. Effective nonfiction readers use inquiry as their purpose and path for learning. The following checklist provides a tool to observe students' inquiry behaviors.

### Acquisition of Nonfiction Concepts

- draws parallels between many pieces of information
- understands and looks for connections between various nonfiction materials

### Nonfiction Reading and Writing Processes

- focuses on important information
- adjusts processing behaviors for nonfiction reading and writing
- formulates researchable, interesting, valuable questions

- generates workable method for inquiry

- accesses material, constructs meaning, reflects upon information

- synthesizes and can explain data

- chooses to read and write nonfiction

- applies learning to new reading and writing experiences

## Attributes

- accepts challenge as part of nonfiction learning

- demonstrates informational knowledge in many settings; dramatic, artistic, etc.

- recognizes the differences between fiction and nonfiction material

## INFORMATION QUEST

This assessment technique puts students into action assessing how they use reference materials, including non-fiction textbooks, trade books and electronic nonfiction text. Asking the students to comment on why they decided to search this resource adds depth to an evaluation of students' ability to be effective nonfiction users.

Create a list of informational tidbits for students to access using nonfiction materials.
Example:

1.  List the oceans of the world in order from the largest to the smallest.

    What resources did you use?

    Why did you use these resources?

2.  What is the Nobel Prize?

    What resources did you use?

    Why did you use these resources?

3.  During what period of history were railroads flourishing?

    What resources did you use?

    Why did you use these resources?

4.  Why doesn't a glacier melt?

    What resources did you use?

    Why did you use these resources?

# In Conclusion

The assessment tools for evaluating nonfiction usage range from an assessment of the qualities of nonfiction material to how effective students manipulate this material. Assessment and evaluation doesn't need to be an added activity. The most productive, indicative assessments are those that occur as part of instruction. Remember, the very best source for satisfaction with nonfiction usage is the students themselves. Ask them to comment on how nonfiction has enriched their lives.

# Bibliography

Begay, Shonto. *Navajo,* Scholastic, 1995.

Coffland, Jack and David. *Football Math: Touchdown Activities,* Pearson Learning, 1994.

Cox, Peg and Neil Morris. *Seven Wonders of the Historical World,* Silver Burdett, 1996.

*Creepy Crawly Collection Series,* Gareth Steven Publisher.

*Eyewitness Books Series,* Darling Kindersley Publishing.

Filipovic, Zlata. *Zlata's Diary: A Child's Life in Sarajevo,* Viking Press, 1995.

Fleischman, Paul. *Big Talk: Poems for Four Voices,* Candlewick Press, 2000.

Fleischman, Paul. *Joyful Noise Poems for Two Voices,* HarperCollins, 1988.

Graves, Donald. *Baseball, Snakes and Summer Squash,* Boyd Mills, 1996.

*Living Spaces Series,* Rourke Publisher.

Long, Jack. *Why is the Sky Blue?,* Forrest House Publishers, 1990.

Machotka, Hana. *Breathtaking Noses,* Morrow Jr. Books, 1992.

Maizels, Jenny and Kate Petty. *Amazing Pop-Up Grammar Book,* Dutton, 1996.

*Make it Work! Series,* Thomson Learning.

Marzollo, Jean. *I Spy Spooky Night: A Book of Picture Riddles,* Scholastic, 1996.

*Mysteries of Science Series,* Millbrook.

Ross, Michael Elsohn. *Wormology,* Carolrhoda Books, 1996.

*Secrets of the Animal World Series,* Gareth Stevens Publisher.

*Weird and Wacky Science Series,* Enslow Publisher.

Wright-Frierson, Virginia. *A Desert Scrapbook,* Simon and Schuster, 1996.

# Reproducibles

# Predicting

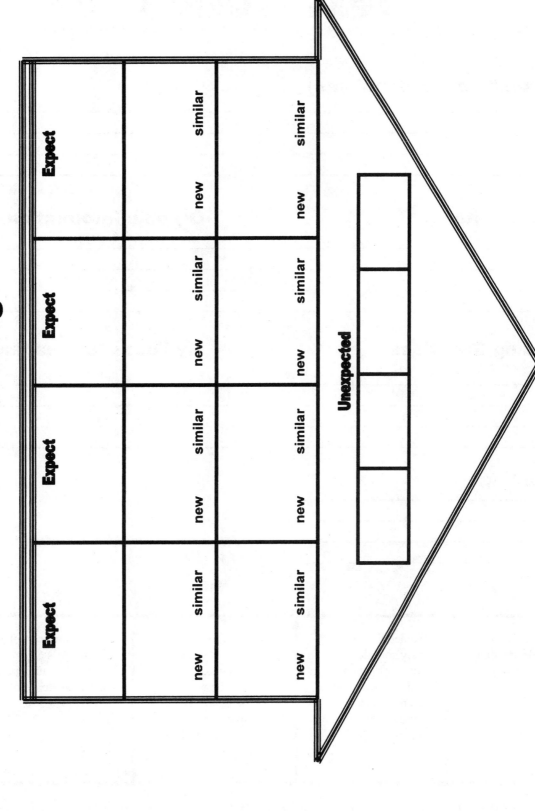

| Expect | | Expect | | Expect | | Expect | |
|---|---|---|---|---|---|---|---|
| new | similar | new | similar | new | similar | new | similar |
| new | similar | new | similar | new | similar | new | similar |

**Unexpected**

# Text Preview

**Lesson/Section Heading(s)**

_____

_____

_____

_____

**Captions**

_____

_____

_____

_____

**Bulleted Items**

_____

_____

_____

_____

**Graphic Information**

_____

_____

_____

_____

**Guiding Questions**

_____

_____

_____

_____

**My Focus for Reading**

_____

_____

_____

_____

**Bold Print**

_____

_____

_____

_____

| 1 | 2 | 3 | 4 |
|---|---|---|---|
| No evidence of understanding or completely erroneous. | -Some/all sections fairly complete<br>-May or may not be in student's own words, when important<br>-Limited evidence of understanding | -All sections complete—some may be sketchy<br>-In student's own words, when important<br>-Some evidence of understanding | -All sections complete<br>-In student's own words when important<br>-Shows evidence of understanding |

# Balloon Organizer

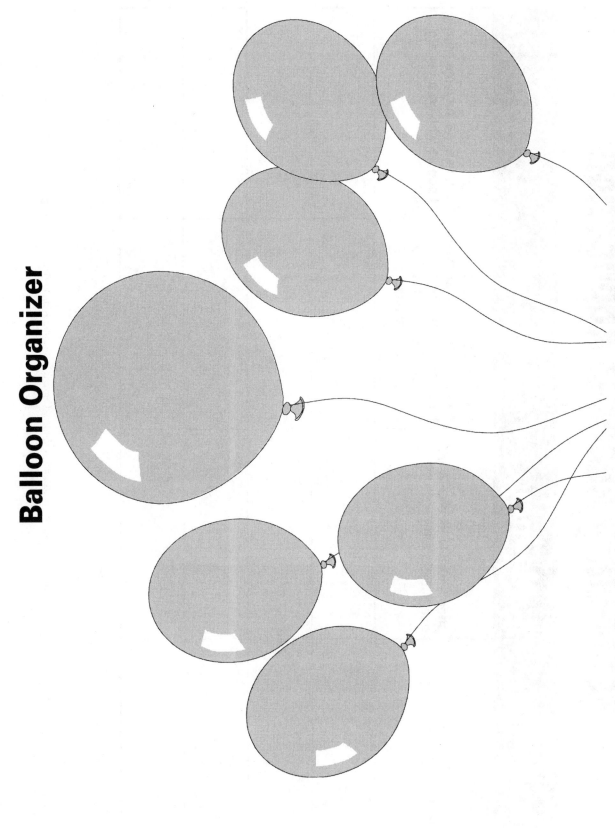

# Vocabulary Analysis Application

| Word | Meaning | Text | Use |
|---|---|---|---|
| Specialist | people who work chiefly in one subject area | Historians today must know how to select the information they need from a huge number of facts.  This is one reason they become specialists. | I can use this anytime I think of people who do a certain job. |
|  |  |  |  |
|  |  |  |  |
|  |  |  |  |
|  |  |  |  |

# Enumeration

**1.**

**2.**

**3.**

**4.**

**5.**

# Time Line/Chronology

**Notes:**

# Magnet Activity

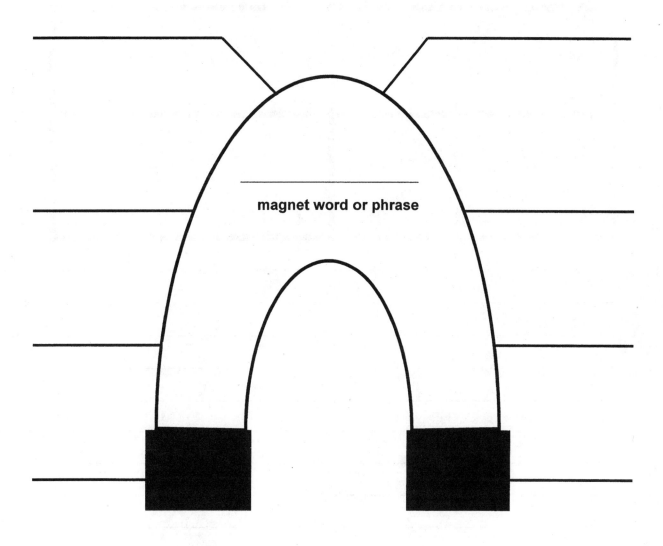

magnet word or phrase

# Magnet Word
## Summary Sheet

| | |
|---|---|
| **1** | **2** |
| **3** | **4** |

_____

_____

_____

_____

_____

_____

_____

_____

_____

# Question Chart

## WHO

Q. _____

A. _____

Q. _____

A. _____

## WHAT

Q. _____

A. _____

Q. _____

A. _____

## WHERE

Q. _____

A. _____

Q. _____

A. _____

# Question Chart

<br>

## WHEN

Q. _____

A. _____

Q. _____

A. _____

## HOW

Q. _____

A. _____

Q. _____

A. _____

## WHY

Q. _____

A. _____

Q. _____

A. _____

# Making Connections

Answer the following questions
after you have read _____.
(Text means what you have read.)

How does the text relate to your
life? _____

_____

_____

_____

_____

_____

How does this text relate to
something you heard about?

_____

_____

_____

_____

_____

What other information have you
read about that helps you
understand this piece of text?

_____

_____

_____

_____

_____

# Making Connections

Answer the following questions
after you have read _____.
(Text means what you have read.)

How does the text relate to your
life? _____

_____

_____

_____

_____

_____

How does this text relate to
something you heard about?

_____

_____

_____

_____

_____

What other information have you
read about that helps you
understand this piece of text?

_____

_____

_____

_____

_____

# Cause/Effect

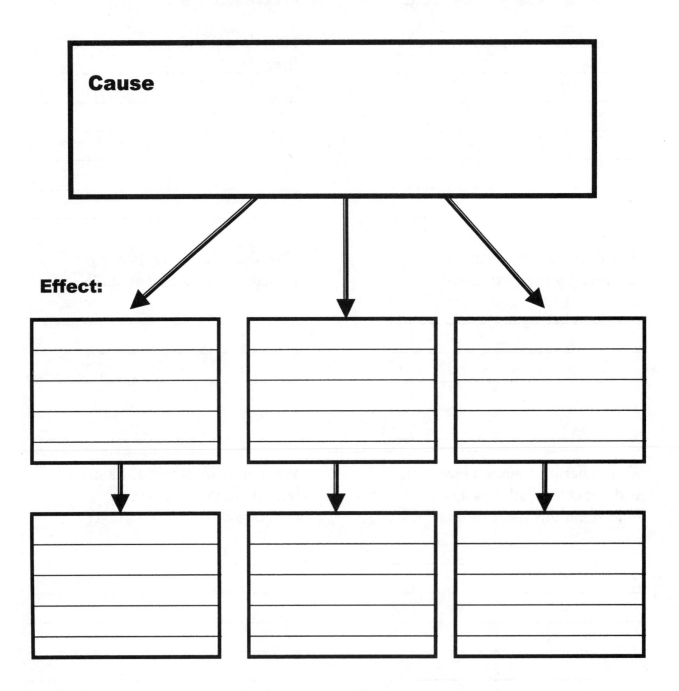

**Cause**

**Effect:**

# Compare/Contrast

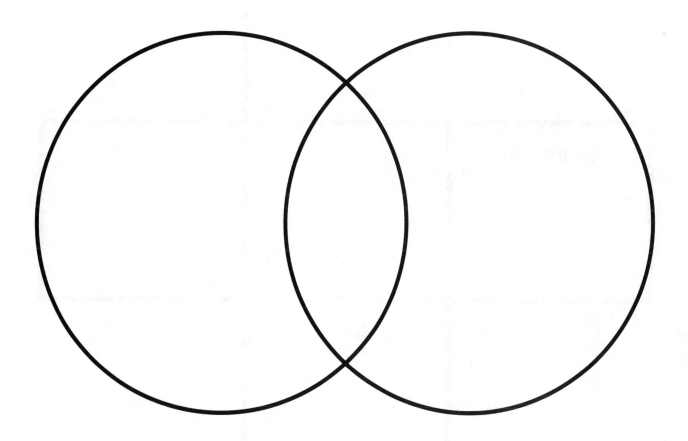

# Definition/Example

| | Example | |
|---|---|---|
| Example | | Example |
| | Example | |

# Question/Answer or Problem/Solution

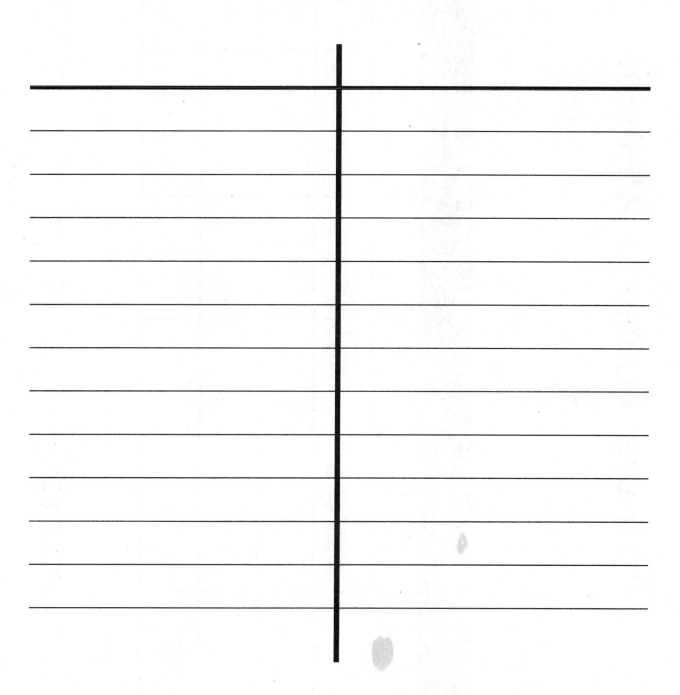

# Authors' Features Analysis

| Author | Experience | Style | Voice | Clear Language | Humor |
|--------|-----------|-------|-------|----------------|-------|
|        |           |       |       |                |       |
|        |           |       |       |                |       |
|        |           |       |       |                |       |
|        |           |       |       |                |       |
|        |           |       |       |                |       |